BEYOND GENIUS, INNOVATION & LUCK

The "Rocket Science" of Building High-Performance Corporations

J. Allan McCarthy

4TH EDITION PUBLISHING

Los Altos, CA

Published by

4TH EDITION PUBLISHING

Inquires should be sent to:
773 Berry Avenue, Suite B
Los Altos, California 94024
E-mail inquiries: Allan@mccarthyandaffiliates.com
Publishing website: www.mccarthyandaffiliates.com

Book design by Caren Parnes, www.enterprisingraphics.com
Edited by Rose Marie Cleese, www.cleesecreative.com

First Edition: November 2011

ISBN: 978-0-9847238-0-5

Library of Congress Control Number: 2011940980

Printed in the United States of America

To my parents, Jack and Virginia,
who are great mentors and always supportive
of my creative ventures.

To my wife and best friend, Laura,
who helped energize this effort with a dose of business reality,
quick wit, and an unusually positive disposition.

To sons Justin and Garrett,
who helped keep life in perspective while completing this project.

Contents

List of Figures   vii

Acknowledgements   ix

Preface—A Little Out of Focus Can Be Disastrous   xi

Introduction—The "Rocket Science" of Building High-Performance Corporations   1

Chapter One—Managing Complex Systems   11
*Planning in a Three-dimensional Context /
what should be on leadership's radar / symptoms of misalignment*

Chapter Two—One Organization, One Blueprint   45
*An artist's rendition is not enough / why plan integrity is important /
defining the elements of a strategy and a Master Plan*

Chapter Three—Sequence: The Linchpin of Organizational Effectiveness   73
*The dilemma of 200 number one priorities / finding the sequence /
imperative sequencing*

Chapter Four—The Difference between a Team of Leaders
and a Group of Leaders   91
*Teaming issues are endemic at the top / team building is not a love fest /
stages of team development*

Chapter Five—The CEO Killer: Misunderstood and
Mismanaged Stakeholders   115
*The power and influence of stakeholders / the increase of stakeholder power /
how to identify and manage the stakeholder landscape*

Chapter Six—Designing a Scalable, Stable, Productive Organization   129
*How productivity is impacted by organizational change /
the wrong and right reasons and times to reorganize / rules of design*

Contents (Cont'd)

Chapter Seven—Calibrating Leverage, Needed Investment,   165
and the Value of Functions

The yin and yang of idea mobilization / determining a function's
value proposition / a functional value worksheet / list of business functions

Chapter Eight—Creating a Culture That Attracts and Retains   179
Talented, Passionate People

What company culture is / how culture creates company context /
creating an Employer of Choice work environment

Epilogue—It *Is* Rocket Science   203

Bibliography   213

About J. Allan McCarthy   217

List of Figures

1.1   The Sigmoid Curve   17

1.2   Multiple Sigmoid Curves   18

1.3   Three-dimensional Context for Planning   21

1.4   Dimension One—Strategic Context   23

1.5   Plotting Progress on Mission Sigmoid Curves   25

1.6   Dimension Two—Cross-functional Context   31

1.7   Examining the Mission Cross-functionally   35

1.8   Consequences of Functional Areas Maturing/ Developing at Different Rates   36

1.9   Dimension Three—Functional Context   38

2.1   An End-to-End Planning Outline   53

2.2   A Balanced Scorecard   65

2.3   CTO Group Master Plan   67

3.1   Two Initiatives in Search of a Sequence   79

3.2   Finding the Sequence with an Interrelationship Digraph   80

3.3   Finding the Sequence and Scoring the Digraph   81

3.4   Raychem Thermofit Division Manufacturing Imperative Sequencing   84

3.5   CTO Group Imperative Sequencing   86

3.6   Strategic Initiative Tree   88

4.1   Stages of Team Development   100

List of Figures (Cont'd)

4.2	Team Agreement Alignment Check	111
4.3	Decision Matrix	113
5.1	Stakeholder Analysis—Example One	124
5.2	Stakeholder Analysis—Example Two	127
6.1	Deployment Matrix	132
6.2	10-Step Organization Design Process	143
6.3	Functional Organization	147
6.4	Front-end/Back-end Organization	149
6.5	Modified Functional Organization	150
6.6	Evaluation Matrix	152
6.7	Marketing/Sales Executive Candidate Evaluation	155
6.8	Manufacturing Staff Executive Candidate Evaluation	157
6.9	RACI Decision Matrix	163
7.1	The Yin-Yang Symbol	166
7.2	Determining Value/Investment for Functional Areas	173
7.3	Functional Value Worksheet	175
8.1	GE Performance v. Culture Model	188
8.2	Employee Satisfaction and Excitement Drivers	191
8.3	Employer of Choice Dimensions	195
8.4	Which Perks Are Most Effective in Retaining Top Talent?	197

Acknowledgements

A book is the culmination of a lot of learning: research, thinking, experiencing, and testing of ideas. I've had the good fortune of forming a close association with many colleagues who are insightful thought leaders, equally dedicated to the evolution of organizational effectiveness strategies. These colleagues have been great teachers and mentors—and I have worked in the foxhole with a number of them. I thank them, those named here, and others whom I have failed to remember: Don Chin, Michael Gordon, Carrie Krehlik, Paul Kurchina, Aliza Peleg, Sigfried Putzer, Ike Nassi, Rick Richter, Garry Ronco, Jim Rossner, Clay Taft, Beth Weinstein, and Don Yakulis.

Some of my clients have been memorable and have made a profound contribution to my work. They were open to trying new things and also improved any result I could have achieved with their input, leadership, and experience thrown into the mix. It was a privilege and a pleasure working with these true visionaries over the years: Ebrahim Abassi, Steve Balogh, Ziv Carthy, Anson Chen, Bill Coleman, Rod Couvrey, Charlie Janac, Doug Merritt, Dennis Siden, Alan Thompson, Joe Weber, Simon Williams, and Mark Yolton.

Several consultants, many with their own respective consulting firms, have been a key source of ideas and learning. I have enjoyed the opportunity to be associated with such bright, talented people who include: Bill Alper, Todd Hewlin, Jim Holley, David Liu, Carol Piras, John Radford, Gary Selick, Jim Wiggett, and Liz Wiseman.

Any author knows that to translate a manuscript into a book is no easy task. An infusion of expertise for editing and book design is always necessary. I've had the very good fortune to be associated with

Rose Marie Cleese, editor extraordinaire and owner of Cleese Creative, who managed the editing aspects of this project. Caren Parnes, owner of Enterprising Graphics, drove the creative elements of the book design effort—which clearly sets a high standard for business book look, readability and feel. A heartfelt thanks to both of you.

I thank you all.

A Little Out of Focus Can Be Disastrous

*You can't depend on your judgment
when your imagination is out of focus.*
—Mark Twain

In 1990 the Hubble Telescope was launched into deep space orbit. This $1.5-billion investment, which represented the best technology at that time, was to provide views of distant galaxies, stars, black holes, and planets unlike anything seen in the past. The first images sent back from the Hubble were out of focus—so much so that they were virtually useless. It turned out that the primary mirror that concentrated incoming light on a digital receptor was too flat, throwing the focus off by 2.3 micrometers (many times less the width of a human hair). One might think that this minor misalignment wouldn't have such a big impact. In reality it was a disaster. Months later, the crew of a NASA space shuttle mission replaced the defective mirror (at great cost) and the rest is history. Images coming from the Hubble are beyond expectation. For the first time we have views of areas such as the Eagle Nebula, believed to be a birthplace of stars. (To view some of these remarkable images, go to www.nasa.gov/mission_pages/hubble/main/index.html.)

The Hubble experience provides a great metaphor for the thesis and content of this book. Today's organizations are horribly complex systems. As such, a lot can go wrong even if an organization has the best and brightest workforce. In the case of the Hubble, it was discovered that a third-party contractor apparently hadn't made the main mirror to specification. This also raises the question about why this mistake didn't surface and wasn't fixed prior to the telescope being placed into orbit by the NASA space shuttle—exponentially increasing the cost to fix the problem. Figuratively, when an organization operates even slightly out of focus bad things happen—loss of productivity, loss of profits, and possibly even catastrophic failure. No matter what size, an organization is expensive to set up and run. Given the complexity and dynamics in which today's businesses operate, it is often difficult to determine when and if misalignments exist—or if something is clearly awry—so that management can put its finger on the exact problem and go fix it. In fact, it's likely that the problem isn't one thing, such as the mirror that was too flat on the Hubble. More than likely, it's a variety of contributing factors that generates misalignments in the first place—misalignments that get lost in the speed and complexity of a company's environment. Even small misalignments that go undetected over time can cost an organization big bucks as they rattle through the deployment side of the workforce.

More than half of the businesses that fail do so, not because of the viability of the technology, product, or service, but rather due to the inability to efficiently mobilize ideas and create and sustain traction in the market[1]. (Note: all footnotes in this book are located at the end of their respective chapters.) Technologists cringe when they hear this. Many myopically believe that the best technology always wins and will overshadow all organizational ills. Years ago, I ran the Internal Consulting Group at Raychem Corporation, renowned for its brilliant scientific minds, innovative products and solutions, and dominant niche markets in defense, telecommunications, and utilities. After touring the Thermofit heat-shrink tubing manufacturing plant, I wandered out to the back of the facility to find 50 large bins filled with defective and rejected product. Most of these discards occurred toward the later stages in the manufacturing process. These discards were, of course, the most expensive types of throw-away that one can experience in manufacturing, since these were nearly completed products (labor and materials were a complete loss). When I questioned the plant manager about this, he replied, "Yeah, we throw away a lot of stuff but our profit margins are nearly 60% and we have 20-year patents that protect our market. We always make up any loses on the front end by inventing new things to sell." That was the corporate attitude, philosophy, and practice, and it had all served Raychem well for many years. But, eventually, it caught up with them. Due to unanticipated competition from expiring patents, plus SG&A[2] running above 40% and thus poor stock performance, Raychem eventually became a takeover target. Tyco became the new parent in the mid-1980s.

Raychem is an example of an organization loaded with the best and brightest minds. But the weight of poor operational practices built into its DNA made it vulnerable to shifts in market conditions—which eventually became its undoing. Architecting the right business platform and fundamentals to mobilize ideas isn't necessarily as exciting as creating new products and markets, especially for entrepreneurs who have been chasing a dream product or service. But the reality is that if the business architecture isn't constructed and managed well upfront, it undermines the creative process of even the smartest, most-driven people.

Over the course of working with many entrepreneurs in my practice, I have had some of them say to me that "the future happens when you're planning for it [laugh]"—meaning that formal planning processes would only slow them down. In fact, some stated to me that they might miss a window of market opportunity if they became bogged down in planning. My observation is that entrepreneurs as a group are some of the best natural planners. Unfortunately, the planning occurs in their heads—in the shower, at breakfast, in the car, brainstorming with colleagues, every waking moment. They are thinking deeply about vision, market opportunities, competition, sources of funding, start-up dynamics, and ways to enter and gain traction in a market. Entrepreneurs become obsessed with the technology, product, or service concept to the exclusion of all else. This obsession or deep thinking is the holy grail of innovation—extremely difficult to replicate in the environments that lost it during the scaling process. (Note: many organizations have difficulty sustaining the spark of innovation when the original founders or idea generator depart, because their innovative thinking doesn't become part of the organizational DNA.)

For some of these entrepreneurs, a company they've begun eventually grows to join the membership of the Fortune 1000. But the outcome for many is not so glorious. Some entrepreneurs hit the wall, so to speak. Their innate planning system (i.e., do it in my head) becomes eclipsed by the needs of the organization. The entrepreneur doesn't recognize this until he or she has already run the burgeoning enterprise into the ground; out of funds, out of time, out of credibility, and not positioned to compete, they witness their market windows open and close. It's likely that, as the new business scaled, the demands placed on the organization (and the plan under which the organization was operating) quickly overwhelmed management's grasp on and ability to effectively lead the entity. Many factors—such as the addition of new leaders and employees; distributed decision making; obligations to investors; introduction of new cultures, time zones, and geographies; increased competition; market and economic pressures; and combinations thereof—created a tipping point that began to pull the organization apart at the seams. As you can see, the list is long. In the end, the ability to plan and execute an early-stage business drifted out of focus for the lack of two things: a clear operating context and key tools or methods to manage the growing complexity and dynamics of an evolving organization.

Mature organizations find themselves in a similar situation: without the right elements in place to efficiently articulate direction and mobilize ideas as a cohesive organization, misalignments are spawned on multiple levels. Misalignments might include: a lack of agreement on direction or an inability to articulate next steps, internal friction and competition among leadership, inefficient resource deployment, and/or an organization structure that doesn't support strategic direction.

Organizations are much more complex in many ways than the Hubble. The Hubble is an inanimate object. It took great technologists and an array of scientists, engineers, and supporting professionals to create and launch this device. In the end, the Hubble wasn't out of focus. It was the organization that created the Hubble and launched it into space that had undiscovered misalignments—which ultimately created a major failure and required significant funds to fix.

Running an effective organization from early stage to mature *is* rocket science. I have great respect for those CEOs and associated executives who step up and lead: forging new industries and conceptualizing and inventing business opportunities to expand product and service availability. Following a hospital board meeting, a board member who was a cardiologist said to me, "I'm glad all I have to deal with are hearts. These are a lot simpler to fix than organizations." He was referring to the organizational complexity that he had just witnessed in the meeting: union negotiations, resetting of the vision and mission, misaligned executives, pressures of fierce price competition, needed reorganizations, etc. He realized how daunting the challenges were.

My thesis is very straightforward: organizational misalignments occur on multiple dimensions spread along the continuum of planning to execution. These misalignments can be difficult to detect and correct with traditional planning methods or algorithms—and stem from a lack of focus. As philosopher Alfred North Whitehead once said, "It requires a very unusual mind to undertake the analysis of the obvious." In this book, I first set out to sensitize entrepreneurs, leaders, consultants, and practitioners to the dynamics in play that create organizational misalignments (which can occur in early-stage and mature companies alike). I call this "managing in context." And, not so surprisingly, like all living things, organizations too have three dimensions to them—three dimensions to be tuned in to and managed. I then share updated methods and processes that help prevent and correct organizational misalignments. These methodologies have been developed over the last 20 years of my consulting work that spans more than 200 companies and 15 industries. Although I'm not one of the hi-tech, innovative geniuses whom I've supported as clients, my contribution has been to decode and articulate what it takes to run an effective organization. This has been my passion and interest throughout my working life.

Your business may have more than its share of geniuses, it may be incredibly innovative, and you might have the "luck of the Irish" on your side too. Those are all great ingredients for success, but I suggest that these are usually not sufficient to grow and sustain a highly profitable business over the long term. There is a high probability that your organization, right now, could be more productive and profitable. This book will help you find out if you are leaving money on the table. It will refresh some old concepts, introduce some new ones, and provide an operating framework that will help position any business for success in both the short term and the long term. I will explain, in practical terms, how to address the "rocket science" of building a high-performance corporation.

I wish you much success in your business endeavors. May you always stay in focus!

Best regards,
Allan McCarthy
November 2011

Preface Notes

1. Mark Ingebretsen. *Why Companies Fail: The 10 Big Reasons Businesses Crumble, and How to Keep Yours Strong and Solid.* Crown, 2003.

2. SG&A: Sales, General, and Administrative expense that is considered overhead; normal SG&A for this industry was 22%.

The "Rocket Science" of Building High-Performance Corporations

*The complexity of contemporary states seems to
break down any single mind that tries to master it.*
—Will and Ariel Durant

Silicon Valley in California, epicenter for numerous early-stage to mature global organizations, is littered with the skeletons of failed businesses. These businesses were likely founded on a combination of genius, innovation, and luck. If the lack of great ideas and smart people wasn't their primary downfall, what killed them? In all likelihood, these businesses failed because of the inability to profitably mobilize ideas over time. Like the Hubble's misaligned mirror, many organizations have built-in misalignments or defocusing elements that are enough to cripple them—draining productivity and profit. When management fails to proactively surface and address current and potential misalignments, this is what I call a management disability. For example, a disability could be that the executive leadership of a company is not working together as a cohesive team—and even occasionally being publicly antagonistic

toward one another. As a result, there is internal competition for resources, as well as a power struggle over the direction of the business.
All too often, the employee population can observe this dynamic at
play (as measured in annual employee survey results). A disability of
this nature can become devastating when leaders are incapable of ac-
knowledging the huge impact it has on the organization at large and
not stepping up to deal with it. A blind spot of this type generates a
ripple effect that permeates organizations on many levels.

*"There are many opportu-
nities for organizations to
operate out of context..."*

Sadly, the leadership example I noted
above is much too common in the business landscape. And, while this type of
leader behavior can significantly impact
an organization's viability, morale, and
ultimately, its productivity, there is a much more deadly and latent leadership disability lurking in the fabric of many organizations: managing
out of context. Chapter One, "Managing Complex Systems" is devoted
extensively to this topic.

There are many opportunities for organizations to operate out of
context: old planning methods (or planning algorithms), clashes of per-
sonalities and cultures (i.e., human nature), shifting competitive pressures, or a changing product or service landscape. These conditions put
pressure on the internal workings of an organization and can create or
exacerbate existing misalignments. But most types of misalignments are
not only predictable but can also be prevented or, at a minimum, proactively managed—if an organization's leadership is inclined to do so. Note
that I say "inclined to do so." Addressing misalignments could mean
confronting an ongoing rift in leadership or possibly disrupting the status quo to better align headcount and resources with the current business
need. Not fun "have-to's."

Most organizational misalignments fall into categories that I term "ineffective management." In other words, these misalignments are well within the control of leadership and, if recognized and proactively addressed, likely preventable.

Eight chapters, eight key elements that help companies soar

I have identified eight categories that provide the key to preventing situations like The Hubble Syndrome from occurring in most organizations and the key to building and leading a high-performance corporation; these eight categories form the chapters of the book:

1. **Managing Complex Systems**

   In Chapter One I define the three distinct dimensions of organizational context that leaders must be aware of and manage: Strategic, Cross-functional, and Functional. This is not a philosophical discussion. Each dimension has different aspects to it and requires a different mindset and planning algorithm to effectively manage it. Planning for each (initiatives, decisions, and actions) must be conducted in the context of the other two. Not doing so guarantees that misalignments will be embedded into the DNA of the organization—which is likely the most common leadership mistake that I have witnessed as a consultant.

2. **One Organization, One Blueprint**

   Most organizations, whether small or large, have some sort of plan. And the tendency is for functional areas to carve out their piece of the plan and go do it. This certainly creates focus and some degree of measurable output—but not necessarily aligned, efficient, productive output. In most organizations, there is a significant opportunity to reexamine and refine the planning algorithms used to define and deploy workforce activity and other resources. When the correct techniques are used, the right resources at the right time will be focused on the right things—leveraging time and money.

3. Sequence: The Linchpin of Organizational Effectiveness

    Organizations rarely have a formal process for determining plan sequence. Planning generally centers on priorities. There is a very big difference between these two concepts and the related activities. To use the metaphor of building a house, the architect and head of construction don't speak about priorities—the conversation is focused on sequence. It's not possible to build the roof on a house if the walls are not constructed. This same logic applies to companies. We get bogged down in leadership debates (politics at its best) about priorities (initiatives, projects, and resources) when the discussion should be centered on identifying the optimal sequence in which to queue up work activity—ensuring that a strong, sustainable organization is being built. A discussion about organizational priorities is generally moot because this activity can lead to false-positives in planning—and can resource-starve critical activities in the growth and development of an organization.

4. The Difference between a Team of Leaders
    and a Group of Leaders

    The topic of teaming and team building has been beaten to death in literature and certainly during consulting interventions. It's hard to find a leadership entity that hasn't experienced some sort of team-building activity. And yet, the quality and competence of leadership teams leave a lot of room for improvement. We don't need to like each other to be an effective team (although it certainly helps), but we need to make sure that the basics are in place and operating well—which can be extremely difficult to achieve at the executive level of many organizations. Inefficient teaming at the top is a key source of organizational misalignment. While it is not easily fixed, understanding the principles of effective teaming and striving to that end will yield a significant, positive impact.

5. **The CEO Killer: Misunderstood and Mismanaged Stakeholders**

I have worked with many CEOs and C-level executives who doomed their tenure by this single blind spot: stakeholder management. A CEO once remarked to me, "Manage stakeholders? I sit with them every month at board meetings. That's enough." Hardly. Recognizing the internal and external stakeholder landscape and proactively managing it is the difference between success and failure for many executives. Even if the company direction, products, and services are exactly on mission, stakeholders who have misperceptions about the various aspects of the operation can quickly derail an executive career. Check *The Wall Street Journal.* On just about any day you can find an article about a displaced C-level executive who may or may not have been performing to plan—but likely became fodder for a news story for not performing to the known or latent expectations of stakeholders.

6. **Designing a Scalable, Stable, Productive Organization**

It appears as though shuffling boxes on an organization chart has become a cure for all company ills. Poor performance? Reorganize. Leadership issues? Reorganize. Product quality low? Reorganize. In fact, organization structure has little to do with these ailments. Shifting organization structure, however, is one of the most disruptive activities an organization can undertake. If typical workforce productivity is 72% and drops to as low as 43% during a significant change event[1], then one would think that this tactic would be used sparingly, saved for those "absolutely needed" situations. Yet, this practice is common. I am aware of companies that reorganize routinely every six to eight months—and of course complain about productivity, poor employee retention, and a lack of strategic focus.

7. **Calibrating Leverage, Investment, and the Value of Functions**

Each organizational function (Sales, Marketing, Product Development, Human Resources, Finance, etc.) has a specific value and leverage that it provides to the organization at certain points in time. Understanding this contribution, or what I call "value proposition," and investing correctly at the right time and situation are paramount. For example, if you underinvest in R&D, you might not have the next generation of products ready as current offerings commoditize or reach end-of-life in market. There must be dynamic management of functions—a give-and-take if you will—as opposed to entrenched organizational fiefdoms that operate as though they are profit centers and businesses unto themselves. And I find the classic concept of the yin-yang useful to help understand the natural tension that exists between investing in R&D and innovation versus putting in place organizational elements needed to successfully commercialize ideas. This discussion helps unlock and leverage various functional disciplines that tend to get neglected as a business scales.

8. **Creating a Culture That Attracts and Retains Talented, Passionate People**

In this day and age, it's not enough to have the best vision or the most innovative ideas. People and organizational culture matter like never before. The ability to assemble a cast of talented players and keep them focused on company imperatives is essentially the ultimate competitive advantage. However, it's not as simple as paying great salaries or having the best benefits. Friday donuts and a lunchroom TV are nice but far from what's needed to compete for today's highly mobile and eclectic millennial workers. So

> *"...a dynamic company culture provides the forum and catalyst for achievement."*

what is? It's the ability to create and operate a dynamic company culture that provides the forum and catalyst for achievement. Say hello to the Employer of Choice century. Companies that don't get it and can't create it will watch their great visions, technology, and other innovations wither on the vine—lacking sufficient people power to compete in the marketplace.

The content of this book is based on empirical logic, unusual in-depth experience, piercing wisdom extracted from "been there, done that" clients, and common sense. Most of what I present should be familiar to those of you who have managed a business—but I've set it in a conceptual framework that will systemically help you to identify and describe the key levers for running and scaling a business, from early stage to mature. Make no mistake, as I noted earlier, this is rocket science. The power of this methodology comes from setting a comprehensive operating context and using effective, yet simple, tools and planning algorithms that are designed to keep pace with the needs of today's dynamic, global businesses. While it is relatively easy to understand, it isn't necessarily easy to do.

To help translate this discussion into meaningful, proactive action, each chapter includes tools and techniques that I have successfully applied in a variety of real-world situations. My hope is that you can take what I have learned, add your wisdom and experience, and translate this into impactful action for your respective business setting.

How this book came to be launched

A bit of history about me will help you understand how it was that I came to sit down and write a how-to book about building vibrant organizations that are highly effective at taking ideas to market—and what gets in the way. Following graduate school, I spent the early chapters of my career as a business consultant working as part of an external management consulting firm. Our mission was to help move failing companies out of the red and into the black. My specialty was front-end analysis. In this role, I preceded the main consulting group to the job site by two or three weeks. My goal was to conduct an analysis to determine 1) the degree to which the vision and mission had been articulated, 2) if the workforce was actually implementing plans aligned with the documented strategy, 3) if leadership was flying in formation and executing on the same agenda, 4) if the organizational structure supported the strategy, and 5) if the workforce contained the necessary capabilities in the right locations to, in fact, carry out the plan. Upon completion of this analysis I would present my (high-level) findings to the combined key company executives and principal consultants of the main consulting team. This input was used to craft a transition road map for putting the company back on track—and hopefully on a path to profitability. Many times our solution included a sizeable workforce reduction, which was painful for all involved. I personally viewed myself as an organizational surgeon. If we didn't take out the unnecessary headcount, then the organization would fail (the patient would die) and *every*one would wind up with no job. In many cases, it was hard to figure out what caused the organization to reach the point it did. Wasn't there a way to prevent the human carnage and run a company with a more efficient, profitable organizational model—one that would allow the company leaders to proactively envision and respond to change as opposed to having to subject the company to an outside consultant's axe?

Over the course of almost two decades during which I worked with those 200-plus companies in over a dozen industries, I received the greatest business education I could have ever hoped to attain. My clients, for better and worse, were my teachers. My instructional material was the real-life dynamics of struggling businesses (early stage to mature). My measure of success was the acceptance and implementation of my recommendations. Hopefully, the recommendations and the

"Wasn't there a way to prevent the human carnage...?"

ensuing intervention created the desired result. In reality, it was immaterial. When the consulting firm departs, to some degree the accountability for success goes with it. Many consultants have witnessed the power of the Hawthorne Effect[2]. In some cases this was the advantage that we needed to help restart and re-energize an organization and break the leadership out of its unsuccessful methods of management.

After many years of working both as an external and internal consultant, I began to observe patterns in organizations that indicated likely success or failure, efficiency or inefficiency, cost-effectiveness and profitability or waste and embedded competitive liability. Ironically, years of this front-end analysis work hyper-sensitized me to these patterns of misalignment or inbred organizational disability, so much so that I reached a point in my career where it became almost intolerable for me to work as an in-house employee. As an employee, one becomes locked into its hierarchy somewhere within a function, which makes it very difficult to surface and act on cross-functional organization misalignments with regard to programs or initiatives without appearing to have a political or self-aggrandizing agenda. As the saying goes, "You can't be a prophet in your own land." Acting as an outside consultant, I have been able to help companies more easily and quickly attack those issues that compromise organizational effectiveness—whereas someone internal may not be positioned to drive a similar agenda.

I don't profess to have all of the answers, but in realizing that organizations of almost any size and nature are very dynamic, complex systems, I've become aware of the need for companies to divest themselves of traditional planning methods—methods that have not kept pace with the needs of 21st-century businesses. In this book, I have set forth clear concepts and concrete tools that, combined with the reader's knowledge and skill, can add crucial elements to building a high-performance corporation.

Introduction Notes

1. Prichett & Associates. *Study on Impact of Change & Transition on Productivity in Work Sessions.* 1999.

2. Hawthorne Effect: an increase in worker productivity produced by the psychological stimulus of being singled out and made to feel important, i.e., consultants interacting and observing employees can improve performance.

 **Chapter One**

Managing Complex Systems

A bad system will beat a good person every time.
—W. Edwards Deming

Organizations are systems that grow in complexity as they scale. When one part of the system isn't working well the other parts are ultimately impacted too. It is necessary to think of an organization as having three dimensions that must be simultaneously managed: 1) Strategic, 2) Cross-functional (combined leadership of functional groups, such as Sales, Marketing, R&D, Engineering, Manufacturing, IT, Finance, Human Resources), and 3) Functional. I call this "managing in context."

If this larger context that I'm describing isn't specifically on leadership's radar screen and overtly managed, then a company can become a breeding ground for misalignments related to direction, decision making, resource allocation and deployment, and endless internal politics and conflict. In other words, it is extremely typical for leaders to think and act in one or two dimensions. Why is this a problem? Each dimension represents only a portion of the larger whole or context. Applying leadership discretely to one dimension out of context with the other dimensions invariably sets organizational misalignments in motion that can be counterproductive to the direction and objectives of the organization. Here are two examples to illustrate the point.

An example of managing out of context

A number of years ago mountain lions presented a huge issue to Arizona ranchers. The lion population grew by supplementing its normal food source, deer, with the ranchers' livestock. At some point the ranchers could no longer handle the associated financial losses caused by the hungry predatory mountain lions. The ranchers initiated a campaign, approved by local government, to reduce the lion population and a price per pelt was awarded to hunters. Soon the lion population was not only reduced but virtually wiped out. With no natural predators remaining, the deer population exploded, competing with livestock for grazing rights on the prairies. Eventually, there were so many starving deer that these animals started eating less-desirable foods such as plant roots, bushes, and tree bark. This type of feeding destroyed the natural vegetation. Trees and bushes that held the soil died and didn't grow back like grass would do. When winter rains came there were no plant roots to hold the soil. The topsoil was washed away and the land became a moonscape, damaged beyond repair. The deer population finally died out for lack of food. The ranchers' businesses collapsed because there was no grass left to feed the cattle. The economy of the territory was severely impacted: unemployment peaked and several smaller cities became ghost towns.

> *"...the environmental balance was irretrievably upset."*

The mountain lion culling story above presents us with a very clear example of how taking an action out of the context of a larger system can yield unintended results. In other words, the lions, deer, ranchers, livestock, and plants were part of an ecosystem that, if not kept in balance, was likely to deteriorate. In this case the environmental balance was irretrievably upset. By the time the ranchers realized that over-hunting the lions could lead to a new set of problems (with more severe consequences), it was too late. Unintentionally, the ranchers destroyed their own livelihood.

Another example of managing out of context

A large European-based telecommunications company set a goal to reduce expenses and operate its internal IT function at the lowest-possible cost. This included: employee-issued computers, company work stations, servers, software, and IT support. The entire IT function (for a division) was outsourced to achieve cost reduction targets. A third-party vendor was selected to provide IT services with the goal of reducing costs by $12 million or about 5% of the company's overall IT budget. Almost immediately, employees experienced a reduction in IT service support and slower server response times for software engineering; in addition, less-than-state-of-the-art PCs were issued as part of the third-party vendor agreement. This IT action was a pure cost-cutting initiative that did save money on the functional dimension—actually millions of dollars globally. However, decisions related to this cost-reduction initiative (driven from within a myopic Functional Context) did not address the IT organizational needs as they related to the big picture.

Examining the situation from a "managing in context" viewpoint, we can see these additional Data Points surface: on the strategic level (Dimension One, part of the Three-dimensional Context for Planning discussed later in this chapter), creating and maintaining a state-of-the-art IT environment was deemed mission-critical to product development, market positioning, and partner relationships. On a cross-functional level (Dimension Two), a key goal had been identified to develop an Employer of Choice-type work environment in order to attract and retain the best and brightest IT talent. Having state-of-the-art IT equipment was part of that strategy. The net result of the action conceived and implemented in Dimension Three, which was out of context with Dimensions One and Two, was that it drove away key talent, reduced software engineers' access to servers from home (due to third-party-provider security and firewall issues), and raised the level of employee frustration in the environment.

Antiquated IT equipment that was slow and hard to use was issued with the new money-saving IT contract. This became an embarrassment in front of key clients who expected this entrepreneurial Silicon Valley-based software company to be a role model and on the "bleeding edge" in its use of new technology. So, while approximately $12 million was saved in annual IT direct costs with this new outsourced program, there was an undesirable cause-and-effect set in motion: trim the IT budget to bare-bones dollars and lose productivity, key talent, and company brand in the process. It's hard to quantify or put in finite terms but you can bet that the original cost savings achieved by the IT function were lost many times over in employee disruption and reduced productivity. This single misaligned initiative created enough turmoil and distraction in the workforce to become a tipping point toward decline. Employee defection rose to double digits. That same company's engineering group is still underperforming today and it is a safe bet that this out-of-context IT program significantly contributed to the underperforming environment. Ironically, the IT functional leader thought that he was doing the right thing—and to this day probably thinks he acted and is acting in the best interests of the company. He likely even received a healthy annual bonus for exceeding the $12 million cost savings. Unfortunately the converse is true. The actions taken were out of context and severely damaging to the organization as a whole, its momentum, its employee attraction and retention, its productivity, its morale, its image with customers, and ultimately its profit. Why couldn't leadership see this phenomenon playing out in the environment? Leadership wasn't "managing in context." Functional leaders were in the habit (without penalty) of acting in the best interests of their own functional agendas—rather than considering the larger company context.

In the examples above, taking actions out of context of the larger system or organization can lead to unwanted outcomes—which can translate to poor productivity and a negative impact on profits.

Unfortunately, a typical organization is a much more complex system than the situation that existed in the Arizona case described above. This is why I term effective management of today's modern, global organizations "rocket science." It is not enough to be a great entrepreneur or great leader or great technologist or the best service provider or the best manufacturer of products. At the end of the day, leaders of modern organizations must have the capability to manage multi-dimensionally complex systems—able to think in three dimensions concurrently, not just one. And, as mentioned earlier, we need 21st-century planning algorithms (systemic planning routines) that can address both the complexity and speed of our modern-day organizations. We need to understand and manage not only the larger context or ecosystem in which our companies operate, but we also need practical, efficient tools to make sure that, internally, organizations don't bog down and drift out of focus in these complex systems.

In this chapter I will describe "managing in context." To do so we need to tune in to what I have labeled Three-dimensional Context and use this as a mental model for overtly managing a 21st-century organization. Let me state upfront that I am well aware that business environments are not linear in nature. There are many forces at play that prevent firms from a single-minded straightforward approach. Leaders need to think dynamically and act concurrently on many levels. This is also exactly to my point. If companies don't manage in a multi-dimensional setting (or have the ability to do so), then they are likely making mistakes—unaware that they are setting themselves up for bigger problems down the road.

I should note that a common complaint about anything labeled "planning" or conceptual in nature is that "while you've got your head down planning, the future just happens." This implies that planning is a form of paralysis that really distracts leaders from what is important. The key phrase here is "head down." You don't need to put your head down and lose focus on the "big picture" or critical activities that are in motion to plan. The opposite can be true. By using the correct methodology, you not only keep your head up but you also become sensitized to the dynamics in the macro environment in which the organization is operating. This promotes effective decision making and the implementation of actions that are most impactful (in context) for the organization. The ranchers who exterminated the lions and touched off a series of unwanted events are a great example of how the implementation of programs and initiatives that are out of context with the larger system can lead to disaster. The ranchers might have predicted the outcomes and taken a different course of action—if they had been properly equipped to deal with a complex system issue.

> *"You don't need to put your head down and lose focus on the 'big picture'..."*

Current planning models are inadequate. Refining these models a bit and clarifying operating context allow us to promote the necessary in-depth thinking, to get the right minds with the right knowledge working on and solving the right issues and to make sure that this all happens in the right context. This will yield a dramatically different result. Let me introduce you to the Three-dimensional Context for Planning.

Planning in the Three-dimensional Context

Charles Handy[1], a futurist, introduced a theoretical model for how any organism begins, grows, matures, and then dies. Handy's model, the Sigmoid Curve[2] (Figure 1.1), showed that for organizations there is inception, growth, maturity, and then decline.

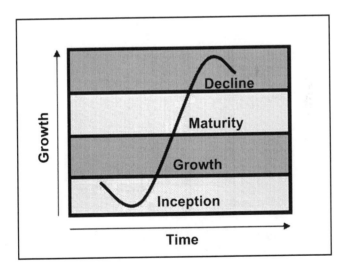

Figure 1.1: The Sigmoid Curve

Applying his model to the business world, Handy noted that organizations typically have many of these growth-and-decline curves during their lifespan and that the trick is to understand when an organization has matured in a given cycle (I call these cycles "missions") and then design and transition to the next mission prior to the decline. Handy emphasized that management does not want to wait until a period of decline to start figuring out where to go next. That is a time of layoffs, cost-cutting, and divestitures. It's not a pleasant time or the best juncture to think deeply about next steps toward the future. This is generally a firefighting mode during which rationale decision making goes out the window.

Handy also pointed out that it is very counterintuitive to rethink your business and architect the next curve or mission during that period when you're successful (at point "A" in Figure 1.2 below), taking orders and making money. But that's exactly when the planning for the next curve should occur.

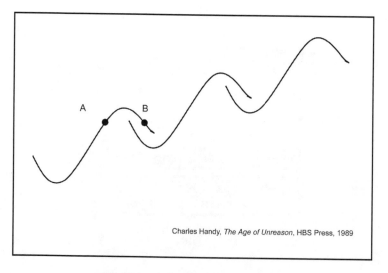

Charles Handy, *The Age of Unreason*, HBS Press, 1989

Figure 1.2: Multiple Sigmoid Curves

The Sigmoid Curve analogy is a great planning tool. I've challenged many leaders to plot where they thought their business was on the Curve

(Figure 1.2) and, after they picked a spot, asked them how they knew, in an attempt to identify the specifics on which their observation was based. Next, I would work to sort through the evidence that led them to their conclusion: point "A" (growth and maturing), point "B" (somewhere in decline), or somewhere else on the curve. This model has also served as a great alignment exercise after my having a similar conversation with each C-level executive, one on one, and then having everyone compare and discuss the results as a team. As you might suspect, it was typical that results didn't match up 100%—which provided a good business case for working on leadership alignment—and refining the planning algorithms of the company.

"...the Sigmoid Curve analogy didn't accurately reflect the complexity and organizational dynamics at play..."

Over the years and many companies later, I began to realize that the Sigmoid Curve analogy didn't accurately reflect the complexity and organizational dynamics at play in a typical company. In fact the model itself could prove misleading because it didn't describe the complete operating context embodied in a typical company. In order to create a complete picture, I evolved the Sigmoid Curve analogy into what I call the Three-dimensional Context for Planning.

The Sigmoid Curve model is generally used to represent what is going on in the strategic dimension. Running parallel and somewhat invisibly are two other dimensions: Cross-functional Context (the leadership team represented by the typical functions of Sales, Marketing, Product Development, Services, Human Resources, Finance, etc.), and Functional Context (actions that are driven within and by a specific function, such as Sales). Thinking on all three levels of context (Strategic, Cross-functional, and Functional) concurrently prevents situations such as the Arizona case or the Telecommunications IT case, both examples of severe organizational consequences caused by out-of-context decision making and actions.

Disciplining ourselves to think in three dimensions

Consciously thinking about an organization operating in three dimensions prevents decisions and actions from being taken out of context, one of the largest sources of organizational misalignments. Thus, the purpose of this Three-dimensional Context for Planning is to create a mental model and a conceptual approach to thinking and managing an organization as an interrelated system—and knowing that decisions and actions need to be made in context, from strategy to execution. This helps ensure that all of the variables in motion (strategic plans, organizational structures, key initiatives, decisions at every level, resource allocation, product road maps, employee acquisition plans, location strategies, etc.) are carried out in the same context aligned with the ultimate purpose and direction of the organization—in synchronization with one another and complementing one another.

Deliberate definition and management of a systemic operating context are where an organization wins or loses the ability to create and sustain focus at multiple levels. The cumulative effect of subtle organizational misalignments (scattered across the organizational landscape) are what create the drag on productivity and profitability. Leaders need to realize that embedded misalignments in the organization's operating fabric exist naturally and that it is their job to capably navigate through these.

Let's take a look at the Three-dimensional Context for Planning model (Figure 1.3) below:

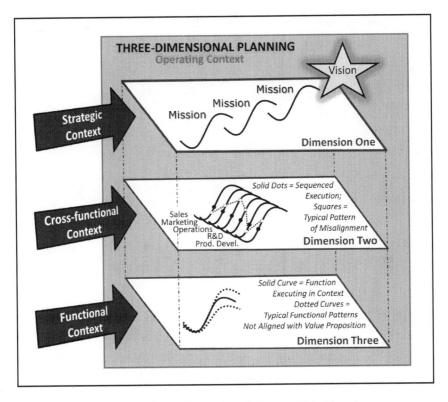

Figure 1.3: Three-dimensional Context for Planning

Figure 1.3 shows the complete conceptual model for the Three-dimensional Context. The three dimensions are: 1) Strategic Context, 2) Cross-functional Context, and 3) Functional Context.

In essence, while an organization embodies and operates as though all three dimensions are one, it is important to pull the Sigmoid Curve apart and acknowledge that there are three discrete dimensions and that each dimension supports and interacts with potentially different stakeholders, and different needs and requirements, all working in different sub-contexts. Each dimension offers a unique but only partial point of leverage in achievement of an organization's strategy. This cross-dimensional awareness, thinking, and ultimately vetting of thinking, decisions, and actions is core to the concept of the Three-dimensional Context. When viewing the operation of an organization holistically, as an interacting system, one finds that it's easier to discover and contain misalignments that occur (intentionally or unintentionally) in the normal course of business. For example, it's not okay for the CTO to create a technical road map without the necessary input, buy-in, and vetting with the stakeholders embedded in the other dimensions. It seems simple enough in theory. Yet, it tends to be extremely difficult in practice. It's important to recognize that an organization has three dimensions in play, all part of the same system, all inextricably linked, all in need of concurrent management to achieve organizational effectiveness.

Dimension One: Strategic Context

Leaders should be thinking about the ultimate direction or vision, the current mission, and the high-level objectives or imperatives that need to be accomplished to get there. Anything articulated at this level is dynamic. While these strategic documents serve as the overarching context for the organization today, assumptions on which the strategy is based may shift quickly and even be precipitated by forces outside of a company's direct control.

Organizations of any kind are formed for a reason, a purpose. This is articulated into a vision statement that describes at a high level why the organization exists, where it's going, and what it's trying to accomplish over the long term. In some respects the vision may not be achievable even in the distant future, for example, "cure world hunger." John F. Kennedy created a vision for America in 1961 that was to "put a man on the moon and return him safely home by the end of the decade." A vision provides a larger context, a point of focus or guiding light, in which to rally and aggregate action. It is important that the vision is compelling and understandable, thus easy for others (especially employees) to comprehend and buy into the effort.

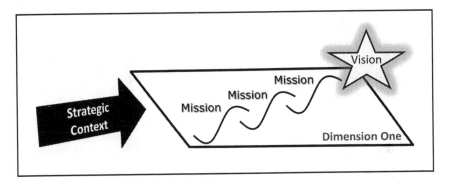

Figure 1.4: Dimension One—Strategic Context

An organizational strategy also includes a Mission Statement (represented by each Sigmoid Curve on the model) which breaks the high-level, long-term vision down into what the organization will focus on achieving over a shorter time horizon (Figure 1.4). As an example, if our vision statement is "cure world hunger" our Mission Statement might be to "abolish malnutrition through advanced farming techniques in Latin American countries in partnership with UNICEF." The achievement of this mission doesn't cure world hunger but moves us closer to that end point or vision. The mission should include high-level objectives, which I term "imperatives," to give investors, stakeholders, shareholders, employees, potential employees, leaders, and others a visceral feel for core areas where the organization's resources will be focused in the near term to complete the mission.

In Figure 1.4 above I have used multiple Sigmoid Curves to represent separate 18- to 24-month missions that progressively move the organization toward achievement of the vision. It would be extremely unusual for an organization to have articulated more than one Mission Statement in advance (in great detail). Companies that have been in business for a number of years are able to plot the mission progression over time. This can also be a very enlightening activity for an executive team to perform. In the telecommunications industry one such mission was "development and implementation of wireline phone services to the home." This focus was on fixed or wired phones. The next curve or mission was "mobile phones for all." The current mission for the converging industries of telecommunications and data communications is "anytime, anywhere broadband access" (voice, messages, and video over wireless and wireline devices).

> *"...an executive team is not synonymous with a visionary or a visionary team."*

It is easy to draw and discuss Sigmoid Curves and speak theoretically about the placement of point "A" and point "B" and when to shift from one curve to the next. It takes a very astute leader/leadership team to read the tea leaves of the industry, market, and competitive environment and best judge how and when to make these organizational shifts: where to invest, where to focus, and when to jump to the next curve. Stating the obvious, that's also why the leaders make the big bucks. Sometimes it takes a crystal ball or an extraordinary human being to envision the future and create a path toward it. Figure 1.5 (below) is an example of how to use the Sigmoid Curve as a strategic visioning tool.

Challenge your management team (if a leader) or your client to define the past mission or missions and current mission of the company and plot on the curve the company's progress to date. What evidence supports these observations? How far forward is the planning team able to project in terms of plausible mission curves? How do you know? At what point does the organization need to prepare for and jump to the next mission curve? I've had clients say, "We're definitely at point 'D' because we achieved these high-level objectives over the last two years, the industry has shifted, and now we're ready to design and transition to a new mission." Then a tremendous debate spontaneously erupts as the executives work through individual perspectives, arriving at a consensus of complete disagreement. A key here is to remember that an executive team is not synonymous with a visionary or a visionary team. This observation shouldn't be construed as good or bad and it's not intended to offend any reader. It's a statement of reality. While it's healthy for an executive team to voice perspectives and noodle with concepts, just make sure that the vision and the next mission are articulated by the true visionary(ies) and not by the democratic method or by committee. That would be a certain kiss of death.

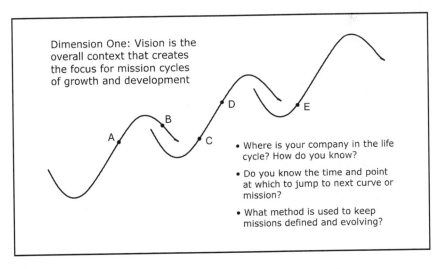

Figure 1.5: Plotting Progress on Mission Sigmoid Curves

At the end of the day, the Three-dimensional Context discussed here is a conceptual model: a tool to guide critical thinking and scenario planning and to refine strategic thinking over time. Of course, there is no one right answer. There is, however, an appropriate level of in-depth thinking that needs to occur with and in the right minds to generate visions and missions. It's common for organizations to be in danger of not giving this topic enough periodic attention.

Dimension One: What should be on leadership's radar

Here are five key elements that are important to get right when addressing this dimension of planning:

1. Make sure that the vision is articulated and refined so that someone outside of the company would be able to read and understand it. In addition, make sure that the mission is clear and includes six to ten imperatives (core areas of organizational focus over the next 18 to 24 months) spelled out.

2. Make sure that visionaries within the company are on board and involved in periodically reviewing the vision and in particular, adjusting the mission as necessary. Note: Many times the visionary is the founder (or co-founders) who departs when a company is acquired. It is also typical for product, technology, or service visionaries to be located in positions other than that of ranking executives. It is important to identify and include these individuals when necessary. If no visionaries are on board, it is vital to have a "Plan B" for how to acquire this critical input. Techniques might include: innovation panels with industry thought leaders, the enrollment of board of director members for the specific purpose of visionary expertise

in the chosen industry, and/or retainer contracts with known visionaries (non-competitive, of course) in the market space.

3. Involve the right people in any planning activity. Think beyond hierarchy and include those key individuals who represent thought leadership and the future of the company. Scenario planning is a great semi-annual activity in which a larger group of key individuals can be incorporated in the planning process. Scenario planning is "what if" planning that challenges baseline assumptions and predicted outcomes.

    For example, when I joined Komag, Inc., a media manufacturing company, in the late 1980s, I asked the CEO when he anticipated the hard media (hard disks in disk drives for computers) business to commoditize. The floppy disk drive industry had commoditized a few years earlier, destroying the cost-volume-profit model virtually overnight. Few companies were left standing in the off-shoring and consolidation aftermath. The CEO's face turned beet red with emotion as he said, "Media production is as much an art form as a science. It's about gigabits per square inch. Sputtering is an art and we're good at it. It will never commoditize like the floppy industry did." I joined the company when its stock price was $35. One month later ReadRite, Inc., came out with a data compression technology that exponentially enhanced data storage (by compression) on the existing hard drive medium. The industry changed overnight. After about 14 months, when Komag's stock stopped its free-fall, it was worth about $4. Komag filed for restructuring under Chapter 11. I wanted to say "I told you so!" to the CEO, but the next time I saw him he was pushing a dolly cart through the Komag parking lot with his office contents on it heading for his car. He was done and it was time to move on. Scenario planning (discussed in "Chapter Two: One Organization, One Blueprint") may not have helped to predict the ReadRite technological breakthrough that turned the media business upside down, but it might have helped Komag proactively position itself to better handle the radical commoditization event. In technology, it's bound to happen at some point. Bringing to mind the old tried-and-true adage, "hope for the best, plan for the worst," I say "plan for the best and plan for the worst." Doing so, an organization will have a shorter reaction/response time when something unplanned happens or will possibly foresee what is likely to come.

4. Make sure that a Mission Statement is crafted clearly and is translated so that the average employee can understand it. This document should be reviewed quarterly for any changes that might impact the underlying planning assumptions, such as changes in market conditions, competitors, economy, technology, etc. The quarterly review should calibrate the progress the organization is making on the Sigmoid Curve. Consensus isn't critical. What is critical is that a) a discussion occurs, b) to the best of the ability of the planning team, a determination is made about progress, and c) the implications of this discussion are communicated to the leaders of the organization so that all other planning activity involves these data as the guiding context.

5. Key objectives or imperatives (primary areas of company focus for all activity) need to be created in support of the Mission Statement and then sequenced. A detailed discussion of sequencing is the focus of Chapter Three.

Symptoms of misalignment

As in all dimensions, there are a lot of things that can go wrong. Here are some obvious examples of misalignments:

1. *No visionary on board and/or no mechanism in place to refresh and refine the vision over time.* It's possible that the visionary (who is likely the company founder) has moved on. The organization is now run by skilled leaders who are not visionaries. This is a disability that can be addressed in a number of creative ways as mentioned earlier, but the bigger issue is recognizing that being the CEO or CTO or other C-level executive doesn't necessarily mean that you have visionary capability. This is an extremely complex issue that is at the root of the downfall of many organizations.

2. *Inability to understand inflection points in the Sigmoid Curve life cycle (where your company is on the Curve).* It's a bit of a guessing game. Where are you relative to the life cycle of the organization? Where are you in relation to the evolution of the market, your competitors, and where you'd thought you should be according to plan? Since it's not an exact science, the best you can do is to pay attention to this issue and spend adequate time discussing and reflecting on it with the right minds involved. Anything less is too high-risk, given the stakes. In addition, this gaining of input from significant others (board of director expertise, internal expertise that is otherwise lost in the hierarchy of the company, and other stakeholder expertise) is one of the best ways to leverage these key players who are part of the organization and whose input would otherwise go untapped.

3. *Inability to translate the vision into an actionable mission and inability to translate the mission into imperatives.* Many organizations operate with a vague strategy and seem okay with it. Other organizations craft a clear Mission Statement and implement it from beginning to end without any flexibility, without fail. This approach might be worse than having a vague

mission. While a mission needs to be specific, it also needs to flex to the dynamics of the real world. In other words, use it as the context or a way to test that all actions are in alignment. But don't think for one minute that shifting conditions can't invalidate some of the assumptions on which the plan is based.

4. *No mechanism in place (scenario planning/business intelligence) to ensure that the vision/mission is refreshed and relevant.* This needs to be a programmatic activity. As an example, SAP Labs had several employees devoted 100% to traveling and taking the pulse of the competition, customer needs and wants, and market trends. One could argue that it's impossible to adequately monitor all aspects of the competitive landscape in this fashion. However, this investment in resources served as a catalyst and forcing function to make sure that periodic scenario planning sessions were conducted.

5. *Stakeholders not aligned on direction (the "CEO Killer").* I've devoted Chapter Five to this topic but it's worth mentioning here. If stakeholders, such as major share holders, board members, and possibly key customers, don't understand the company's direction and to some degree buy in and support it, trouble is at hand. Even with the "right" company direction defined, unsupportive stakeholders can quickly become a leader's undoing. I've witnessed several strong-headed CEOs become a casualty before plan implementation. This speaks to the need to make sure that stakeholders are actively engaged and included in the development of the vision and mission in a progressive fashion. You don't want to wind up in a missionary role. Remember that many times the missionaries were eaten by the natives before they could convert the natives to a prescribed religion or ideology.

Dimension Two: Cross-functional Context

As noted earlier, a single Sigmoid Curve used to analyze the dynamic operation of an organization is simply too compressed. In the Cross-functional Context graphic (Figure 1.6), I have taken a single curve or mission and pulled it apart into the functional areas charged with achieving the mission. This cross-functional dimension is usually synonymous with the leadership team or C-level team. It is in this dimension that human nature (in the form of power and politics) comes into play in a big way, and thus the need for explicit understanding of the variables in motion and what each functional discipline is contributing to the cross-functional agenda.

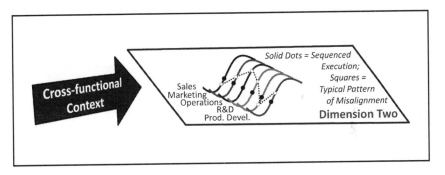

Figure 1.6: Dimension Two—Cross-functional Context

It is important that this cross-functional team understand (interprets the same way) the functional plans and how these interrelate in support of the mission. Ideally, leadership is working together as a high-performing team as opposed to a reluctantly aligned group of functional experts (the topic of Chapter Four) and the plan is based on sound methodology (the topic of Chapter Two). It is very common to find that members of an executive team believe they are in complete alignment on strategy, yet management at successive levels down the organization's hierarchy sees great disparity in how this leadership team is actually executing on that very same agenda. For example, a company conducted a pulse survey for a newly integrated leadership team that consisted of both parent company and acquired company executives. Trying to dispel the perception that a cross-functional leadership team that had been working together for a year was in conflict in and disagreement over the mission, a pulse survey was administered to evaluate the degree to which the leadership team was perceived aligned or not aligned by employees. The results were predictable—and telling: while the top team believed that it was 100% aligned on strategy, the next management level down (direct reports to the top team) responded that it perceived the executive team to be about 71% aligned. Employees three and four levels removed from the executive team said that leadership appeared to be about 52% aligned on overall direction. In this circumstance, as in many organizations, the executives lived in a political environment. They weren't a team per se but had learned to disguise their behavior when in a team setting so as to appear aligned, but acted differently when running their own respective functional areas.

Dimension Two is that point at which a cross-functional leadership team needs to drill-down into a single Sigmoid Curve or mission and translate this into a company plan. So, it's critical that this cross-functional team have an in-depth understanding about how to mix and leverage the power of functional competencies to wring out the best performance for the organization. While this seems straightforward on the surface, there are many ways that this effort can get derailed and yield a sub-optimal result. A key one is that many functional heads who are part of the top team (cross-functional leadership dimension) aren't interested in what other functions have to offer. Sound familiar?

Dimension Two: What should be on leadership's radar

These are six areas that are crucial to get right when dealing with this dimension:

1. While "leadership" or "executive team" is generally the label, it is critical that it is in fact a "team" that is driving Dimension Two. The root ingredients necessary to constitute a team are common objectives and explicit interdependencies. As will be discussed in Chapter Four, if a true team has not formed and is not leading at this Dimension, then all bets are off in terms of discussing optimal organization performance. By the way, team building has little to do with fun events, wine tasting, or ropes courses, although these can all be great socialization activities. However, in reality, creating a powerful team includes these components: a) the right players with the right competence, b) common objectives, c) explicit rules of engagement, d) a method for making and vetting decisions, e) a process for managing conflict, and f) clear interdependencies tied to compensation. This has little to do with friendship, fun, and likes and dislikes. A disproportionate amount of energy should be invested here until a "team" is in fact leading the organization.

2. It is important that the cross-functional team that is leading at the Dimension Two stage has a deep understanding of the organization's strategy as articulated in Dimension One. This includes support functions, such as IT, Finance, and Human Resources. That way, all functions are aligning their respective efforts toward the macro level goals of the organization. While this may seem obvious, I can tell you from a consultant's perspective that it is common for key executives to have a very different interpretation of the organization's strategy. All agreeing

on the strategy is helpful but not necessary as long as all action is aligned; all understanding the strategy is critical and a lack thereof is a common debilitating agent in the leadership ranks.

3. It is important that the cross-functional leadership team have a common plan or master plan (crafted) and use this as the road map for creating functional level (Dimension Three) plans and actions. Again, this may seem obvious. Many times leadership teams are what I term "loose federations" that aren't interested in working lock-step or that feel confined by a plan. (A master plan format is suggested in Chapter Two.) What's key is that all moving parts of the organization—from strategy to execution and from financial plans to resource allocation—are accounted for (deliberately managed in context) and not lost in the speed and complexity that are a part of a typical organizational setting.

4. From my consulting experience and in observing the demands confronting many of my clients, I had an epiphany. I realized that organizations spend a lot of time debating priorities when, in reality, this debate is moot. The important use of leader time is to translate a mission into a workforce plan, making sure resources are deployed in sequence, much like building a house. A house is built based on the sequence of what needs to happen first, second, third, and so on. Priorities are not a topic of debate. The same logic applies to organizations. This is covered in-depth in Chapter Three, "Sequence: The Linchpin of Organizational Effectiveness." As you'll note in Figure 1.7 below, the simultaneous missions and the associated actions for each functional area need to be crafted with sequence and alignment in mind. There is an absolutely profound critical path to effective resource deployment in an organization. It's the responsibility of leaders to identify this critical path and make

sure that the functional areas are executing in alignment and in sequence, and pacing resource deployment in a way that gets the organization to an end state in the most productive and efficient way possible.

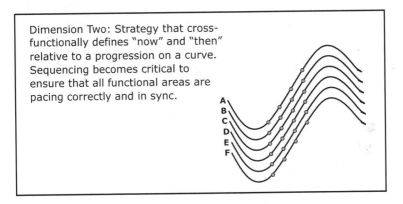

Dimension Two: Strategy that cross-functionally defines "now" and "then" relative to a progression on a curve. Sequencing becomes critical to ensure that all functional areas are pacing correctly and in sync.

Figure 1.7: Examining the Mission Cross-functionally

5. You will note in Figure 1.8 (below) that there is a natural tendency for our strong, driven functional leaders to drift out of alignment. Trying to move out of sequence or get ahead of the other functions isn't necessarily a deliberate action on the part of any one leader. However, I equate executives (the top leaders of an organization) to thoroughbred horses. The tendency of thoroughbreds is to kick, bite, and try to get in front of the herd. This is an innate characteristic of leader behavior. So, it becomes very important that the ranking executive be strong-willed and have the capability to finesse team behavior in a way that keeps leaders working together in a productive fashion—"flying in formation" or "getting the wood behind the arrow," as it were. I've worked with many CEOs who have lamented, "I spent all of this time hiring the best and brightest executives in the industry to help lead the company. Now it's frustrating to find out that I

need to spend a bunch more time trying to get them to work together without killing one another—and be on the same page." Does this resonate? I've also worked with high-ranking executives who have said, "I hired the best and the brightest. I pay them a ton of money. Let them figure out how to work together and get things done. If they can't, I'll find others who can." This is certainly another approach, but not recommended. Teams don't evolve naturally. There are very specific actions that must be taken to promote the evolution of high-performing executive teams. Chapter Four is devoted to this topic.

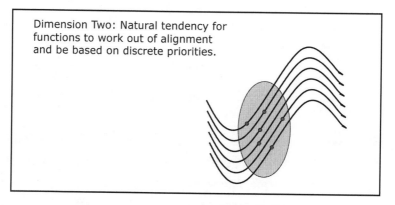

Dimension Two: Natural tendency for functions to work out of alignment and be based on discrete priorities.

Figure 1.8: Consequence of Functional Areas
Maturing/Developing at Different Rates

6. Organization design is a science. Few people in business have specific training in this area. This becomes apparent when witnessing the reasons that organization design and general restructurings are initiated: cost reduction, change in leadership, performance improvement, and accommodation of other organizational changes. While these goals might be positively affected by some form of organizational design, reorganizations should not be the default approach, but rather a supplemental

action taken only after other key factors have been addressed. That doesn't seem to stop leaders from using their favorite tool, organization design, like a snake oil remedy. Got a performance issue? Redesign your organization. Not sure why product quality is poor? Redesign your organization. Experiencing some cost over-runs? Redesign your organization. Not meaning to sound too flippant, but I have seen leaders, over and over again, clearly become stuck on organizational redesign as though it is a cure-all. While redesign alone won't achieve the needed results, it will certainly generate furious activity, clear changes, and a momentary point of focus. Then a leadership team can check off the box and say swift, radical action was taken. In reality, nothing much will have been achieved and more than likely the organization will have lost precious time and productivity with a faux solution. Chapter Six offers a clear, concise methodology for organization design and ways to minimize this highly disruptive activity.

Let's now drill down to the Third Dimension known as Functional Context.

Dimension Three: Functional Context

Organizations of most any size need areas of specialization. In fact, it's a competitive edge to have highly skilled people leading and performing needed work. Even a small startup company might have determined that it needs a CEO (likely the founder or one of the founders), a CFO, a CTO, and possibly a combined business development/CSO or head of Sales. The bane of a small business is trying to balance the addition of specialists with funds available. Without a relative degree of functional competence across the broad spectrum of functions, those functions that are staffed and funded tend to gain traction while other functional areas lag behind. The net result is that mission execution is pulled out of alignment—with short- and long-term consequences (Figure 1.8).

The idea is, of course, to balance start-up needs with spending so that the right talent is added to the mix at the right time. This generates maximum organizational traction (or return) for the invested resources. As an organization adds functions (Sales, Marketing, Finance, Human Resources, etc.), it is adding overlaying functional Sigmoid Curves to the mission. Each functional leader then needs to drive an agenda or sub-mission that is aligned, in support of, in harmony with, synchronized with, and in context with the Cross-functional Context and the strategic context of the organization. While one might think that I'm adept at stating the obvious, I need to emphasize that the taking of actions out of Cross-functional Context is an Achilles heel for many, if not most, organizations. A functional group that is executing out of alignment is problematic. Multiple functional groups executing out of alignment is a guaranteed path to sub-optimization of efficiency, productivity, use of resources, revenue, and profits. I have never consulted with a company where, after minimal analysis, it wasn't obvious that one or more functional groups were misaligned in mission execution.

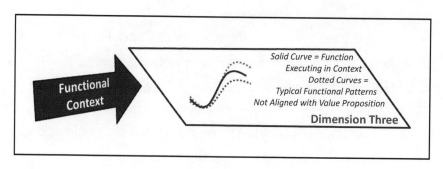

Figure 1.9: Dimension Three—Functional Context

I've used Figure 1.9 as a quick alignment test with a cross-functional leadership team. I ask each functional leader, independently, to plot the key sub-mission milestones for the curve. Then I assemble the team and we discuss alignment. It is amazing to see the disparity between what the functional leader thinks constitutes aligned action versus his or her peers. This serves as an interesting alignment or misalignment awareness building activity, but the best way to make sure that functional curves are aligned and in support of the strategic context is through a consistent planning algorithm as described in Chapter Two.

Looking at Figure 1.9, consider the traits of a misaligned function and how it looks, represented by the dotted curves. It could point out a function that is using a disproportionate amount of resources, given the pace and overall needs of the organization. For example, a sales force might be expanding faster than the ability of engineering to introduce the next generation or suite of products. Maybe the head of Sales is impatient and has started empire-building. In an earlier example, an IT function implemented a cost-reduction program (equipment and service) that undermined the IT needs of other functional groups. Have you ever observed an engineering function that has gone through constant leadership changes and reorganizations as it tries to determine the next generation of products? Have you witnessed a human resources function that doesn't have the right expertise in place to build a competitive total rewards scheme in order to hire needed talent in a competitive market space? Ever experienced a company environment in which a marketing function is not synched up and in support of product development, with the result that communications and branding don't align with the actual products and services? Research shows that a satisfied customer will likely share his or her experience with three to five people. (A dissatisfied customer will tell 10 or more.)

Dimension Three: what should be on leadership's radar

Here are five suggestions to help you ensure that Functional Context is understood and managed well in your organization:

1.   A typical planning approach is for functional heads to create plans and then roll these up for discussion at the cross-functional level—the aggregation of the parts make the whole, so to speak. This moves the cross-functional team to more of a superficial review-and-approve mode. To prevent this dynamic, it's important that the cross-functional team work through a complete planning cycle prior to the creation of functional plans (Dimension Three). That way the planning work performed on the functional level will be done in the context of a plan that was created first in Dimension Two. So, as plans are created and refreshed, the team starts at Dimension One and works down in order to maintain Dimensional integrity. This is important to do because the strategic context might dictate that the engineering group needs to build an eco-friendly hybrid, while the determined head of engineering may push to build a Humvee. Engineering planning needs to be performed in context, not in competition or outside of the preconditions set forth in the strategic and cross-functional plans.

2.   Functional experts, not general managers, should be engaged in and drive planning, especially at the functional level. Not adhering to this may be the most common downfall in organizational planning algorithms, especially in mid-sized and larger companies. Some organizations may tend to favor "a company person" who fits the culture over the expert who may not. Imagine these scenarios: the top executive of engineering who's never designed or coded, the top executive of marketing who doesn't

understand basic branding principles, the head M&A who's an attorney by profession and has little or no experience in acculturation or organization assimilation, a head of Sales who has never run a sales organization, a head of IT who has extensive operational experience but isn't steeped in IT industry trends. Do you see the issue here? Plan integrity is sub-optimized by leader capability. It's imprinted into the DNA of many companies. Also, it is very typical for larger organizations to rotate key talent through a variety of positions in order to develop general managers (and future leaders). This is a great idea—as long as company leaders don't put these individuals in the top functional leadership roles or let them have complete ownership of the planning activity. While true dedicated experts don't necessarily make the best GMs (experts tend to be a bit obtuse), this expertise must be leveraged in the planning process to ensure that the plan that's created has functional integrity. It's not wise to keep functional experts locked up somewhere down in the organization's hierarchy during planning events.

3. Functions are the engines that drive action for any company. As such, they need the right level of resources, people, and money at the right time to make the needed contribution to an organization's agenda. Note that resource allocation needs to be dynamic and may fluctuate given the needs of the business. Because of this, resource allocation must emanate from plan design, not from an executive debate or a constant flow of ad hoc business cases (Chapter Two discusses how to create a master plan with a mechanism for resource loading). In other words, smart people can always make a compelling argument for resources. This debate is a non sequitur and detrimental to

> *"Functions are the engines that drive action for any company."*

effective plan outcomes. An effective planning methodology shows how to mete out resources.

4. Each functional area has a value proposition or contribution that it can make to the organization in support of attaining the overall strategy. A functional area provides value on a continuum of activities. The trick for the leadership team is to determine how much functional value it needs to pay for (not too much and not too little) to achieve the strategy. Chapter Seven is devoted to this topic. Ironically, the value proposition for many functions is simply misunderstood. As an example, if the CEO is a former engineer, he or she might not understand the value the sales function brings to the table and thus under-invest at critical times in this function. Human Resources, a function that historically has had a hard time articulating its value proposition, is commonly under-invested in until companies experience significant employee attrition, leadership, and compensation issues. Ironically, like a sales function, HR is a function that needs investment early on in order to build out scaling infrastructure. Organizations that grow without a defined culture, clear hiring models, people development programs, and so on wind up creating sub-optimal company environments that take a lot of time and money to correct—and even create unrecoverable situations where a market opportunity might open and close but the company is not ready to capitalize on it or simply doesn't recognize opportunities when they occur.

5. As pointed out in the discussion on Dimension Two, it's the functional leader's job to put a company's interests above those that she manages on a functional level. Thus, being tuned into the Strategic Context of Dimension One and the implications this has on how she forms and drives a functional plan (Functional Context, Dimension Three) is critical. Second, and no less

important, a functional leader must fully comprehend ("comprehend" is the operative word here) the Cross-functional Context (Dimension Two) that she serves. It's a delicate balance—but an achievable balance. The functional leader needs to be adept enough in her functional area to interpret the needs of the business, especially at the cross-functional setting, and make sure that the functional team is performing in lock-step with those described needs: not in competition with the larger group, neither ahead nor behind the group, able to pull the right functional levers at the right time.

Summary

I can't emphasize enough the importance of, first and foremost, "managing in context." In the end, we must think strategically first (Strategic Context, or big-picture thinking), cross-functionally second (Cross-functional Context), and then and only then functionally about the tactics (Functional Context) that drive an organization's resources. This approach unlocks the power of systems thinking. What makes "managing in context" so difficult is that all of us tend to gravitate to our areas of interest, that which we do well. This eventuality can taint our leadership judgment. The "specialization" (which is the source of our passion and personal strength for most of us) is what creates the blind spots in our perspective and in our actions.

Abraham Maslow once sagely observed, "When all you have is a hammer everything looks like a nail." If we become sensitized to the fact that we all have a predisposition(s) or preference(s) that filters and skews our thinking and objectiveness, then, with this awareness, we can compensate for this propensity and the accompanying blind spots that affect our judgment to be better architects and leaders of organizations.

The planning algorithms shared in this book help overcome this innate human disability. It's rocket science, no matter how you look at it.

Chapter One Notes

1. Charles Handy. *The Age of Unreason.* 1995.

2. Sigmoid Curve: Many natural processes, including those of complex system learning curves, exhibit a progression from small beginnings that accelerates and approaches a climax over time.

 **Chapter Two**

One Organization, One Blueprint

Every well-built house started in the form of a definite purpose
plus a definite plan in the nature of a set of blueprints.
—Napoleon Hill

An artist's rendition is not enough

Years ago I worked with an architectural firm. I learned that in the construction of a home there are about 16,000 decision points—everything from the style of house, location, colors, and landscaping to the placement of wall switches, faucets, and toilets. The construction begins with the future home owner hiring an architect to discuss general parameters. The architect then creates an "artist's rendition" or a series of watercolors of what the house might look like from various internal and external viewpoints. These initial drawings are adjusted to the owner's desired end state (the equivalent of a company's Vision Statement). Is the architect's work complete? Far from it. Next, the architect creates a series of "blueprints" that addresses, among other things, land surveying and leveling, position and size of the house, types of materials, and colors—all the way down to a blueprint section for each subcontractor who will work on a particular portion of the house, i.e., plumbing, framing, wiring, roofing, foundation, etc.

Why must an architect create such detailed plans when licensed contractors (equivalent to a company's functional leaders) and subcontractors will do the work? These individuals are state-certified in electrical, building, plumbing, foundation, and so on. Shouldn't these professionals be able to create their own plans and do quality work? The answer is simple: although the contractors could certainly create their own plans based on the artist's renditions or even from a high-level, general contractor blueprint of the overall construction, their work would lack the benefit of knowing the specific intent of the original owner or architect (what each or either of them had in mind). In all likelihood, the subcontractors would wind up doing quality work but filling in the blanks or grey areas with their own interpretation of the artist's rendition. The result would be such things as wall switches, although legally installed and safe, in the wrong place; a color scheme that doesn't meet the owner's expectations; faucets and other fixtures that are of high quality but don't match the intended design; and so on. That's why the architect takes full responsibility to think through the vision and translate it into a much more specific plan, thus eliminating room for interpretation by others who didn't participate in the original visioning activity. With detailed plans from which to work, the subcontractors can execute their specific portion of the plan without spending a lot of time trying to interpret the deeper intent of the plan, minimizing additional interpretations that might conflict with what the owner and architect had in mind.

If I now take this analogy and transpose it onto the typical organization, the result is this: the owner and architect are an organization's founder(s) and/or top executive(s). The artist's rendition is a "vision statement." The blueprint created by the architect for the contractor and subcontractors translates to the top management team creating the mission, imperatives, and Master Plan for the organization. The contractors and subcontractors are the heads of the functional areas (Sales, Marketing, Engineering, etc.) charged with the responsibility to execute the plan.

Who is responsible for crafting and translating the artist's rendition into blueprints for the organization? The executive team (and possibly the extended executive team). And, herein lies a key issue where a disconnect can form between the intent of the vision and actions taken to implement the vision. Many leadership teams have articulated only the vision and initial elements of a blueprint prior to delegating this strategic content out into the organization for deployment. What happens when an incomplete blueprint is delegated for execution? A lot of bright, profes-

> *"Imagine all of the opportunities for decisions to be made out of context with the vision."*

sional, dedicated, and energetic leaders, managers, and employees become involved in creating plans—like the contractor/subcontractor example above—that include a huge amount of interpretation that may or may not be aligned with the original intent of the leadership team (architects). What's worse is that the 16,000 decisions required to build the typical custom home are dwarfed by the number of annual decision points that occur in the operation of the average company. I've had CEOs estimate that tens of thousands of decisions points occur in an organization in a 12-month period. And, in large, scaling, and global organizations, the decision making is distributed down the hierarchy and across cultures, time zones, and geographies, exponentially increasing the possibility that decisions are not in complete alignment with the architect's original intent. Imagine all of the opportunities for decisions to be made out of context with the vision.

Generally I think that most employees in an organization want to be successful and perform in an aligned, productive fashion. Without the blueprint, how would they know if their actions were aligned or not? I'm also convinced that many executive teams are happy to create an artist's rendition and stop there. They love to be visionary but don't want to do the heavy lifting it takes to translate that visionary thinking into a blueprint that is much more prescriptive in nature. This may sound like a somewhat cynical observation, but I think that many top leaders are in the habit of "dreaming up stuff" but not that compelled to translate the dream into a more visceral, tangible action plan.

The mobilization of ideas, as I call it, requires very adept thinkers and is as important as the idea generation side of the equation. A great visionary who is incapable of or doesn't have the attention span (or ability) for translating a vision needs to surround himself with very skilled people who do have this competence. Otherwise, there is a high probability that the "brilliant" idea is more like a shooting star…bright for a moment and then goes dark. With that darkness comes a confused workforce, a sloppy and misaligned deployment of resources hooked to a dream that may or may not have a path to success. I also believe that when you think on a topic (a vision) deeply and long enough to translate it into a blueprint that you'll find many times that the original vision isn't viable or might even be flawed. The dream needs adjustment, refinement, or could even be "the bridge too far." This is why handing off a vision without a detailed blueprint that forces interpretation from the visionary/strategic thinkers is a cop-out and sets the organization on a dangerous path as it operationalizes the plan.

What organizational symptoms can be seen when faulty architecture or an incomplete blueprint is in place?

▷ More than 100 number one priorities over which bright executives debate and lobby for resources

▷ An organizational environment in which employees complain about a lack of focus and confusion over direction

▷ An under-performing organization where leaders are baffled about the root causes for this under-performance

▷ Flavor-of-the-month initiatives coursing through the company

▷ Projects and initiatives without clear outcomes, in competition with one another or in conflict with one another

▷ Management concerned about the overall execution and ability of certain functional groups and their respective ability to achieve goals

▷ Constant management complaints about lack of resources

▷ Draconian financial controls implemented at the corporate level to control costs and headcount. If the CEO (and/or his delegates) is counting and controlling headcount, this is a key indication that the business lacks a viable plan.

▷ A clear disconnect between the vision and the deployment of the vision

▷ Rumblings on the board of directors and Wall Street, and among other significant stakeholders about company performance, leadership, and direction

I should note that creating a blueprint that includes a higher level of refined thinking is not micromanaging functions—no more than an architect creating blueprints for contractors and subcontractors is an act of micromanagement. Micromanaging occurs when leaders and managers start doing the job that belongs to individuals one or two levels down in the organization. A common example of micromanaging is when a senior vice president responsible for a $100 million operation and 800 employees needs five levels of approval to hire an employee or spend $10,000 on a project. An executive at this level should be given a budget and the blueprint and then told to "go run your business and execute according to plan. Don't spend more money than the budget allows. Don't hire more employees than the plan allows. Make sure that all of your decisions and actions are taken in the context of company culture and strategy. If you run over budget or don't meet plan, then we've got a problem and so do you—up to and including termination."

Creating a blueprint is the responsibility of leadership and a way to ensure that the organization is genuinely being built and operated in alignment with the strategy. The idea here is not to threaten those charged with leadership responsibility but to empower those key individuals to act within the context of the plan.

Plan integrity is important

A Master Plan shouldn't be in the desk drawer or an obscure document that is referenced only during an annual planning cycle or when a consultant inquires if, in fact, one exists. The Master Plan should be a dynamic working blueprint that is tattered, torn (figuratively speaking, in this new paperless world), reworked, and debated…but always central to any discussion, decisions, and deployment of company's resources. The plan should eliminate any confusion over priorities and reduce the discussion to fine-tuning actions as outcomes are monitored. As Dwight

Eisenhower said, "The plan is nothing, planning is everything." Planning is the process that creates the blueprint and aligns leaders in a common context so that one doesn't need to refer to the plan every minute. The planning process imprints intent in the DNA of leaders and managers—and equally in the employees when properly involved and informed. This is running a business "in context," making decisions "in context," taking actions "in context." And, it is important to have a Master Plan format that includes all of the necessary ingredients to create the magic sauce called a successful organization. Below I describe a Master Plan format, tested in many organizational settings, that can provide a solid operational framework. This can be revised, edited, and evolved to serve the needs of any organization. The overarching point here is to: 1) create a Master Plan, 2) make sure that leadership has thought deeply enough to not only articulate a stable vision but also translate that vision into a blueprint, 3) keep the plan dynamic, alive, and upfront in running the organization, and 4) deliberately discuss and manage across the three dimensions discussed earlier: Strategic Context, Cross-functional Context, and Functional Context. This won't require additional planning time. It will reduce or eliminate countless meetings where managers debate priorities. It will minimize the grey areas in the vision that remain open for functional interpretation. It will eliminate rogue behavior on the part of executives who want to empire-build or operate in fiefdoms. Fortunately or unfortunately, depending on how you look at it, this approach will put tremendous pressure on top executives to "be present" and "participate in" thinking through the strategy and related actions. I call this "teaming"—a foreign concept in many companies. And the biggest deal of all is requiring all top-tier executives to coordinate their calendars and make it a priority to spend quality time together—and get the planning work done prior to moving into a deployment mode.

When an executive team finds it hard to calendar several days together to conduct planning, I say, "Cancel all plans, both personal and business, until the Master Plan is complete. I don't think you want to be known as yet another 'Hubble Syndrome' management team."

In July of 2011, our friends at Cisco Systems announced that the company had lost focus, would retrench, and likely cut 10% to 15% of the workforce (maybe up to 10,000 jobs). While CEO John Chambers was being treated like a rock star in the media for stepping up to these difficult challenges, billions of dollars of shareholder value will have been lost, talented employees dumped onto the street, and both local and foreign competitors finding a golden opportunity to capitalize on market share. There is no mystery here. Cisco leadership fell asleep in managing Dimension One. This algorithm occurs constantly in business: get successful, gain a dominant position, and when leadership believes that the company's success makes it immune to market dynamics, the leader(s) fall asleep at the helm. Oops.

"Cancel all plans, both personal and business, until the Master Plan is complete."

Figure 2.1 (below) shows the end-to-end plan or blueprint and its component pieces that an organization should have in place and use as a blueprint with which to run the organization. Concepts, such as Data Points, sequencing, resource loading, imperatives, and interdependencies will be introduced here. Some of this terminology will be new, but most will not. The power for the organization (to operate efficiently) comes from the ability to manage all of the pieces in a Three-dimensional Context.

I have devoted the majority of this book to explaining the purpose and importance of each piece of the end-to-end plan and how to build and run other critical elements of the organization in support of the plan. Here I will briefly detail the five general sections of the planning outline (Figure 2.1).

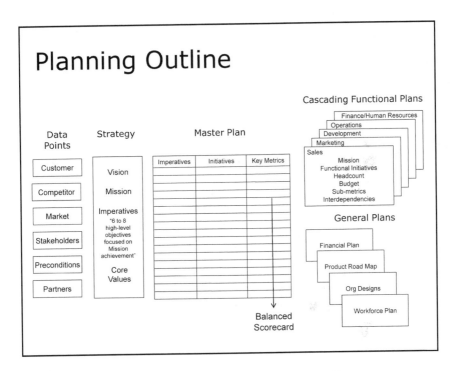

Figure 2.1: An End-to-End Planning Outline

Data Points

There's a variety of reference points that, in fact, has great influence over the construction of plans, tempers thinking, provides context for that thinking, and may even dictate boundaries for organizations. Unfortunately, few aspects of the Data Points are static in nature, which is why planning algorithms must be dynamic. If the conditions on which a plan is based change or if the underlying assumptions change, then it logically follows that the plan itself must change. Even subtle shifts in Data Points can have profound effects on a plan and how resources are deployed.

In this planning outline, I've listed the top six Data Points that I consider relevant. This is not an all-inclusive list. Clients generally will refine and/or add additional Data Points. The six Data Points listed are: Customer, Competitor, Market (or product/technology trends), Stakeholders, Preconditions, and Partners. Examples of other Data Points might be: economic environment, historical company lessons learned, and determination of the value proposition and investment for functions (the focus of Chapter Seven). It's important to make sure that the necessary Data Points are included in any planning activity.

It's critical that the Data Point information is generated and distributed to the planning team before the strategy is created, as Data Points provide critical information and context that will shape the assumptions on which a plan is based and ultimately the planning outcomes.

Years ago I facilitated a strategic planning process for a start-up organization called SmartMachines. The company was attempting to break into the lucrative market of building semi-conductor manufacturing equipment, namely the robotics that operate certain stages of wafer handling. Robotic equipment for this purpose must run in a Class Five clean room (a strict air quality environment) and minimize vibration to the delicate semi-conductor material during handling. At the beginning stages of the planning process, I said to the CEO, Charlie Janac, that the planning team needed to create a one-page synopsis for each of the Data Points. If it took more than one page to articulate the relevant information for each Data Point then it was likely that further work, even research, would be required to ferret out necessary planning insights. Charlie challenged the need to collect stakeholder information. In this case, the stakeholders were five board members and one large venture capital investor. Charlie said, "I'm on the phone every week with these stakeholders and we have a board meeting monthly to review progress. I know these guys very well." Charlie thought that this activity was a waste of time. I said, "Let's stick to the process. I doubt that you've had a direct conversation, one on one, with each stakeholder regarding these questions: 1) Do you feel that we have a clear direction and are executing efficiently to that end?, 2) Is the leadership team performing as expected and on track?, 3) Are there certain expectations that you consider above all else the most important for us to achieve short- and long-term to be considered successful in your eyes?, and 4) Do you have any other guidance, input or concerns?" Reluctantly, as with most executives when given this assignment, Charlie did agree to meet one on one with the board members and the VC. The following week, as we debriefed the experience, Charlie had a sheepish look on his face and said, "There was a consensus among the board members that my CFO wasn't competent in the job and that this was a direct reflection on my ability as a CEO. Most felt that we had overspent on prototyping at this stage of the pre-IPO operation. Most are a little disappointed in my ability to describe the specifics of the plan that we are currently executing and wonder why it's taking so long to get to where we say we are going." Charlie also noted that he received a number of very valuable insights with regard to board expectations. He was surprised that the direct feedback included disappointment in his performance as a CEO. He was under the impression that everything was hunky-dory.

"Most felt that we had overspent on prototyping at this stage of the pre-IPO operation."

There are several powerful points to be emphasized here: 1) stakeholders have tremendous influence over the success or failure of an executive team, 2) stakeholders have critical planning information, including expectations that must be identified and considered early in the planning process (discovered and then documented in the plan) that are dynamic (changing over time) and must remain on management's radar screen, and 3) stakeholder expectations known and/or unknown are likely the most common killer of executives in organizations (figuratively, of course). This third point is the focus of the discussion in Chapter Five, "The CEO Killer: Misunderstood and Mismanaged Stakeholders."

How to create Data Points

The planning team needs to solicit help from the best minds (members both of the planning team and likely outside the planning team—even outside of the company) to generate an information synopsis for each Data Point. All one needs is a one-page synthesis of the relevant information related to each Data Point. Then the planning team can take this into consideration and use this information as important reference points (context) in the creation and refinement of the strategy. I strongly suggest that the Data Points be assembled into a packet and become required reading prior to strategy formulation. Note that some Data Points may be elusive in nature and require expert guidance, e.g., economic trends. With past clients I have had university and government economic advisors participate in a panel discussion to share their perspectives on the topic. The output from such a session is then synthesized on one page—again to provide the best possible supporting information. If arranged and facilitated correctly, sessions of this nature can provide pivotal and timely input, since companies can become somewhat internally focused over time and may lack external perspective.

Benjamin Gilad, author of *Business Blind Spots*, speaks very eloquently to the topic of the need for companies to invest in "intelligence," i.e., dedicated employees who are charged with the responsibility to monitor competitor actions, market trends, government policies, etc., and uncover any information (legally) that may be strategically relevant. Gilad, a former intelligence officer in the Israeli Army, points out that there are vast amounts of information available to businesses that are relevant to strategic and operational decision making, although it's true that finding that information is not so easy. As the title of the book connotes, Gilad contends that business blind spots can be huge competitive liabilities. A little intelligence work can help neutralize or even leverage these blind spots. Raychem Corporation, a scientific-based product organization always funded several "intelligence gathering" senior-level employees to scout emerging markets, global government politics, economic trends, and the like—all acutely relevant to the company's vertical utility and military market segments. These intelligence scouts periodically debriefed their findings with the executive team and even served as an aggregation point for bits and pieces of business intelligence that would otherwise have been lost in the organizational landscape.

On innovation and break-through thinking

I have worked with many organizations that have become concerned about their ability to remain competitive—and to keep on the leading edge of technology, product, and service innovation. As one CEO stated, "We have lost our ability to think 'out of the box' and challenge the status quo."

After many years of inside corporate work and outside consulting engagements in which I supported initiatives related to this topic, I am convinced that break-through thinking doesn't occur accidentally—and there is a specific tactic that can be used to achieve this end.

William Manchester, a biographer who has studied and written about many great people such as Douglas MacArthur and Winston Churchill, said, "All great people appear to have one common characteristic: the inordinate ability to focus on one thing long enough to think it forward—to take it to a new level." I call this "constructive dwelling." My observation is that entrepreneurs, innovators, and inventors display this same characteristic: they obsess, block out the environment around them, and have the inordinate ability to focus on one thing long enough to take it forward to a new level. This magic is many times lost as a company scales and the founder departs.

This break-through magic can be replicated through clever Data Point management, that is, assemble a strategic thinking team of several bright, experienced people, then have them examine existing Data Points and add any new relevant information into the mix. Ask this group to come up with a series of conclusions about a product or service or technology evolution. Periodically, have this team meet and continue this focused thinking (adding new information as it is available), which ultimately will move the thought process forward to a break-through level. Louis Pasteur said, "Opportunity favors the prepared mind." These bright people will be prepared and will recognize and/or define and seize opportunities as they surface.

The lesson here is that through the rigorous use of Data Point management (as described above) we have a tangible way to promote and likely achieve break-through thinking on an ongoing basis—but we must be prepared to recognize and leverage these epiphanies when they surface.

Elements of the strategy

The strategy consists of Vision, Purpose, and Mission Statements, and development of Core Values and Imperatives.

Vision and Mission Statements have been the target of a number of comic strip humorists. Scott Adams, author of the *Dilbert* comic strip, once dressed up as a consultant and facilitated an executive group in the creation of a vision and mission. He didn't tell the group that he was a humorist with no experience developing these pivotal documents. Adams' point was that these documents are rarely meaningful and really a waste of time. To some extent, I agree with him if these documents are simply aspirations and the actions of the organization aren't a direct manifestation of them. This disconnect is more common than one might think, which gives the skeptics and humorists fodder for their forums.

A Vision Statement and a Mission Statement aren't necessary evils. These are pivotal to strategy formulation. And, these terms are not universally used in the same manner by all executives and academics. I think that the humor enters the picture when these strategic elements are simply too confusing and vague to translate into "what do I do when I come in on Monday morning?" Following are the definitions that I use in developing these core elements of the blueprint.

Defining the vision

The Vision Statement should be the artist's rendition, i.e., addressing why the organization was formed, where it's going, and what it will look like when the vision is attained. This can be a lofty goal for the distant future—maybe 10 years out or more. In Chapter One, I quoted former President Kennedy saying, "Put a man on the moon and return him safely home by the end of the decade." A Purpose Statement is a common-sense extrapolation of the vision but speaks to the macro reason for being, e.g., Google's Purpose Statement is: "Google Inc. was founded to make it easier to find high-quality information on the web (1998)." This purpose may evolve over time but is generally very stable in organizations. The vision and purpose must be articulated well enough so that the average employee can understand these. Otherwise, the documents become problematic by not offering necessary strategic context.

Defining the mission

The Mission Statement answers the question, "What are we striving to achieve now?" It is the articulation of one of the Sigmoid Curves or life cycles of the organization and represents what the organization will be doing over the next 18 to 24 months to move closer to the realization of the vision. A Mission Statement for a hi-tech organization could be to "create a converged technology platform so that wireless and wireline datacom infrastructure can seamlessly handle 4G capable devices." If you're not in this business you may not understand the verbiage used above to describe the mission. That's okay. What is important is that all of the employees and shareholders of that business clearly understand this mission and can rally behind it. The Mission Statement also needs to include 6 to 10 key imperatives or the primary areas of focus for the organization during this 18- to 24-month period. The imperatives are high-level objectives, or über-objectives. All projects, initiatives, processes, and programs will need to directly support these imperatives in the Master Plan (discussed next). This provides a clear line of sight between all of the activities in which the organization engages and the key leverage points for achieving the mission. A method for defining organizational imperatives can be found in

The Transition Equation: A Proven Strategy for Organizational Change, J. Allan McCarthy, The Free Press, 1995, or on my website at: http:www.mccarthyandaffiliates.com.

The Core Values of a company do matter

Core Values, another topic that humorists like to target, actually do matter. Research shows that organizations that define and model Core Values (aligned with Employer of Choice criteria[1]) have reduced attrition and a more productive workforce in general. The test of a Core Value is "In difficult times will the organization stay true to its nature and continue to model these values?"

> *"Values are the base on which an organization's culture builds over time..."*

Values are the base on which an organization's culture (all of the behaviors, actions, programs, and processes) builds over time and are extremely difficult to change. Net–net, it's important to know who you are and what you want to become—because every little decision takes you one step closer to that end point, i.e., if you're not clear on the type of culture you want to build, a de facto culture will form—which you may or may not like as it matures.

Here's an example of Lockheed Martin Corporation's Core Values:

▷ PASSION...to be passionate about winning and about our brands, products, and people, thereby delivering superior value to our shareholders.

▷ RISK TOLERANCE...to create a culture where entrepreneurship and prudent risk taking are encouraged and rewarded.

▷ EXCELLENCE...to be the best in quality and in everything we do.

▷ MOTIVATION...to celebrate success, recognizing and rewarding the achievements of individuals and teams.

▷ INNOVATION...to innovate in everything, from products to processes.

▷ EMPOWERMENT...to empower our talented people to take the initiative and to do what's right.

A strong correlation between happy employees and optimal shareholder value

There is statistical evidence that shows a strong correlation between organizations that model Employer of Choice (EOC) company attributes and organizations that tend to generate the best shareholder value.[2] These data have been long in coming. Many believed that this correlation existed through intrinsic evidence. Now, with hard facts in hand, companies are jumping on the bandwagon—trying to use this as a point of competitive differentiation. The EOC attributes that consistently rank as most important are: a compelling company vision, a clear career path, competitive pay and benefits, and great people managers. These attributes are not necessarily listed here in order of importance (the economy and market forces create variability here), but these four attributes have been on top of the EOC list for many years. Anecdotal data also suggest that compensation is continually underrated: its importance in most environments is much higher than voiced by employees. Distant fifth, sixth, and seventh attributes include a flexible and adaptable work environment, a reputation for innovation, and social responsibility, including a spin on "green" or environment. Thus, if you want to create an organization that generates optimal shareholder value, then a bit of cultural engineering is in order (this is discussed further in Chapter Eight). Creating and managing in an EOC environment is a significant paradigm shift (approach to management) for many leaders who behave as though employees are expendable commodities.

The Master Plan

The Master Plan is the blueprint that provides context for all resource deployment in the organization and is the "single source of truth"— meaning that independent activities, initiatives, and programs are not permitted to occur outside the context of the plan. During the course of business it is common for a leader to bring forward a business case for adding headcount or starting a new project or program. These should never be approved without first a vetting in relation to the Master Plan. This helps keep the organization's actions aligned and going in the same direction. Conversely, at the same time, it's important that the organization doesn't create layers of bureaucracy that prevent the ability of a leader to respond quickly to the needs of the business. It's a delicate balance.

Recently the new CEO of Hewlett Packard, in an attempt to rein in costs, announced that new centralized headcount controls needed to be put in place. Actions not included in the announcement (but must logically follow to manage headcount on the corporate level of an extremely large corporation) will be to build an entire bureaucracy on top of the current management structure to control headcount in a 300,000-employee organization. This common cost-control method is a great way to undermine leader accountability, reduce organizational agility in the market, and drive out key talent. My point here is that hiring should be controlled by those leaders and managers closest to the work and charged with the responsibility of carrying out the work.

These managers need to be held accountable to the parameters identified in the Master Plan. Controlling headcount with an overlay of bureaucracy guarantees a poorly deployed workforce. Of course, a solid plan needs to be in place before "accountability" can be managed in this way. When a CEO steps down from his or her leadership role to manage headcount, it is indicative of a corrupt Master Plan.

The Master Plan section in Figure 2.1 shows the skeleton framework and it's important to note that: 1) the Master Plan is preceded by completion of the Data Points and Strategy sections; this provides the necessary working context to create a viable Master Plan, 2) Imperatives provide a foundation on which the Master Plan is built, and 3) all ongoing and in-queue programs, processes, and projects need to be loaded into this framework with expected deliverables, due dates, and measures. This then provides the initial Master Plan structure upon which all downstream planning is built and correlated.

"Controlling headcount with an overlay of bureaucracy guarantees a poorly deployed workforce."

The Master Plan is essentially the working document upon which Dimension Two management or cross-functional leadership is based. It provides the forum and opportunity to test the thinking of peers, a way to determine work queue and to allocate resources to make sure that the house is in fact being constructed in the right sequence (and getting the best bang for the buck). It is very possible at this stage that a critical project or initiative will surface that doesn't seem to fit into the plan. The good news is that the leadership team is able to use the plan as a vetting agent to create visibility into why there is a disconnect. It may mean that the plan has some flaws and needs revision, or more likely, that the proposed initiative doesn't fit the plan. It's a very good day when a management team can say "no" to an investment knowing that it truly will not help the organization move forward. Many times these decisions are made on a hunch, political favor, or troubled uncertainty. The Master Plan should also be monitored with some form of "balanced scorecard"[3] (Figure 2.2) that ensures that customer, financial, business process, and people metrics are considered concurrently in the decision-making process.

Key Measures

Customer Measures	Business Process Measures
• Market Share • Customer Retention • Customer Profitability • Customer Satisfaction	• % of Sales from New Products • Quality Defect Returns • Inventory Turnover • New Revenue/Sales Employee • New Product ROI
Financial Measures • Return on Investment • Profitability (Operating P/L) • Revenue Growth/Mix • Cost Reduction/Productivity	**Learning & Growth Measures** • Employee Retention • Employee Satisfaction • Employee Productivity • % Development Plans in Place • % Performance Reviews on Time

Figure 2.2: A Balanced Scorecard

This is a foundational aspect of systems thinking. Balanced Scorecard monitoring and decision making becomes a low-value and even misleading activity if it isn't being applied within the context of a Master Plan, which happens more often than one might think. Special note: there's a tendency for management to compile priorities and initiatives, synthesize these into an Excel format and then apply a dashboard or "balanced scorecard" to this morass. As you may have guessed, I find this to be unsophisticated and problematic management. The plan looks very official with the metrics added—but the content can be garbage. As the saying goes, "Garbage in, garbage out." There is no reason to look further in many organizational settings to discover why organization performance (revenue, profit, and productivity) is not being attained.

Below is an example of a Master Plan (Figure 2.3) for a newly forming CTO group in a large, complex organizational setting. I have significantly generalized/abbreviated the original plan information to protect company information. The original nine CTO Group Imperatives were loaded into this format and then delegated to each of the six CTO group sub-functional leaders. These leaders and their respective teams completed Functional Plans for their respective sub-function. Next, as facilitator, I rolled all of this information up into a single consolidated plan. That way the CTO executive team could examine each imperative with all of the sub-function initiatives in one section. Milestones and measures (metrics) were then discussed. (Note: in the actual plan each imperative had 6 to 25 initiatives identified following the roll-up activity.)

In summary, the newly formed CTO Group created a Mission Statement and nine associated Imperatives (high-level objectives). These were tested with key stakeholders for initial input and revision. Next, the CTO Group functional leads (six in number) discussed the preliminary strategy work with their respective teams. These sub-teams then loaded into the matrix in-progress and in-queue initiatives. The top team then met and conducted an initial vetting of this plan and reached a preliminary agreement on initiative work, timing, milestones, and measures. I should note that the Group Imperatives were sequenced after identification. So, the appearance of the Imperatives in the final plan document are in a special order or sequenced order. I've devoted all of Chapter Three to this topic, not because it's difficult to understand or perform but because it is a unique activity and highly critical to the construction of an effective Master Plan—and the deployment of resources.

CTO Group Imperatives	Initiatives	Milestones	Metrics
1) Create product strategy with proper stakeholder buy-in	• ASIC strategy • Home Gateway & connected • Common component strategy	• Create stakeholder collateral • Set meeting schedule	
2) Ensure relevant product development units are aligned/ executing on plan	• Product line coordination on the 5-year product road map • IP stack strategy	• Hold product developm't summit meeting for buy-in • Quarterly meeting to test alignment	Note: data removed for better readability
3) Periodically collect market intelligence and incorporate in plan	• Regular meetings with key and prospective customers • Internal stakeholder data collection and info exchange	• Quarterly debrief of various intelligence collected	
4) Determine global addressable market and leverage in vision execution	• Develop ESF and include analyst's input	• Review analysis on 6/20/11	
5) Analyze global technology trends and adjust strategy as needed	• Participate in relevant standardization strategy groups • Meetings with startups, potential partners, acq targets	• Create review forum with technology entity • Facilitate a quarterly review	
6) Develop and maintain a 3rd-party/ vendor strategy in cooperation with relevant business units	• Involve business development in product unit evaluation sessions	• Create plan • Gain stakeholder endorsement	
7) Deliver converged IP solutions that leverage products from multiple product lines	• Develop and maintain network transformation offerings for product groups	• Architect solution • Periodically revise solutions plan and test stakeholder alignment	
8) Build and retain the CTO Group with best possible talent and domain experts	• Provide intern opportunities • Hire two expert consultants to supplement team expertise and leapfrog the competition	• Review intern career track at quarterly ops meeting • Hire consultants by Q2	
9) Create a positive, motivating work environment	• Create a continuous learning environment and flexible assignments	• Assign task force to create draft plan • Revise plan and implement by end of Q2	

Figure 2.3: CTO Group Master Plan

The functional leaders were asked to provide their input with regard to needed headcount, resources, and budget. Each sub-group provided this input, which was then rolled up into a master document. The top team once again met and discussed the result. The conversation that took place was different than those that had occurred in the past. Bartering and flamboyant negotiation was minimized. The discussion focused on "what was the logical, efficient way to build the house (deliver on CTO Group strategy)." After the plan was finalized (with resource loading) the CTO Group leaders met with various stakeholders to test for alignment, gain additional insights, and also address any outstanding issues, e.g., the planning process identified a discrepancy between the work commitment and ability to deliver. Additional resources would be needed or some initiatives would need to be eliminated or delayed. Proactively driving this conversation helped make the CTO Group an effective, powerful internal partner in the organization, et al. The finalized plan did include a number of changes: some initiatives were moved up in the queue and given more resources, some initiatives were killed, others that were required proceeded but with less funding, and some units needed to reduce headcount. This was especially difficult because skill sets were not directly transferable among the CTO Group units. The good news is that since these issues were dealt with with premeditation, it gave the team more time to plot employee transitions. Few employees were left without work. Most wound up in a good career-step transition.

The CTO Group head then took her plan to the top leadership team (as did all cross-functional leadership as part of a larger planning effort). This led to healthy debate on the executive level—a productive debate focused on the best way to build the organization and meet performance targets, rather than a debate based on priorities with the best negotiator taking home the prize (headcount and dollars) at the expense of the organization.

Cascading Functional Plans

All functional areas need a plan that is created after (not before) the initial Master Plan is drafted. Next, functional heads must take the Master Plan to their respective groups and repeat the process described above for each functional specialty. A key element of this work is addressed in Chapter Seven, "Determining the Value Proposition and Investment for Functions." Each function (Sales, Marketing, IT, etc.) has a relative value to the organization, given the organization's life stage. While all functions are critically important to the organization, sometimes a greater investment in one area is more necessary than in another. For example, when an organization is rapidly scaling, it is critical that a significant upfront investment be made in both "recruiting and staffing" and "learning and development." Managers need to be trained in proper hiring etiquette and technique and employees at all levels need acculturation and skill development to perform well in an evolving environment. Otherwise, the organization might quickly wind up with leaders, managers, and employees who don't fit the culture; don't make decisions in the proper context; and doom the organization to a downward spiral of misaligned decisions and actions.

> "...sometimes a greater investment in one area is more necessary than in another."

Functional Plans, just like Data Point creation, should be in the same format and shared across the leadership team. This augments the context in which managers think, plan, and act. If planning activity isn't transparent, it's likely that you're dealing with an organizational environment loaded with fiefdoms. Fiefdoms have kings and queens, and secrecy is one of the stanchions of power for a fiefdom. It is also very important that Functional Plans include "interdependencies." Interdependency means that there is an explicit, mutual need that one function has with one or more other functions. It is important to call these out in the planning process so that there is no misunderstanding about these interdependencies with regard to required participation and support. For example, a sales function may need the marketing function to produce a variety of collateral prior to a sales campaign. If the sales function doesn't specifically call out this requirement and identify the dependency in advance, then the marketing function may not have allocated the necessary time and resources to support the effort. In this case everyone loses. Calling out interdependencies in advance keeps everyone honest, on notice, and accountable to deliver against commitments in the plan.

General Plans

It is obviously important for organizations to have specific plans (General Plans) that are superordinate to all other plans (e.g., Functional Plans) and ad hoc planning activity in order to provide context—a glue of sorts to guide and hold the organization together. See Figure 2.1 for a listing of typical General Plans maintained by organizations. It seems that many times the Financial Plan and associated overall headcount budget take on a life of their own and become an organization's surrogate business plan as opposed to the Master Plan. Desired revenue, profit, and expense are symptoms of many other things that are in place and performing correctly or incorrectly in a organization. So, my suggestion here is to identify what General Plans are needed, the necessary processes to create and refresh these over time, and assurance that these remain in the proper context in the overall planning effort. To further interpret this statement, make sure that the business is run from the Master Plan and that the General Plans are properly constructed and tuned to support the Master Planning effort, not vice versa.

Summary

Imagine an orchestra of 100 musicians performing Beethoven's Fifth Symphony. It would likely be powerful and emotionally moving to experience this in person. Now imagine the same setting with a few changes: only a few of the musicians have the conductor's version of the music score (with slight tempo variations), the conductor is very inexperienced but got the job because he was the best violinist in group, and several percussionists had never played in a large orchestra before. As a member of the audience, you might find yourself rooting for the orchestra to perform well, but even feel embarrassed at times when hearing missed notes and periods of out-of-synch play. I give you the modern-day shareholder who invested in a company that isn't well-schooled in, shall we say, the rocket science of building and leading a high-performance corporation.

I'll close this chapter with a relevant quote by Bernard Baruch, advisor to presidents Woodrow Wilson and Harry S. Truman: "Whatever failures I have known, whatever errors I have committed, whatever follies I have witnessed in private and public life have been the consequence of action without thought."

Chapter Two Notes

1. Employer of Choice criteria generally include these
    elements: Affiliation, Direct Financial, Indirect Financial,
    Career, and Work Content; an EOC model is described
    fully in Chapter Eight.

2. *100 Things You Need to Know: Best People Practices for
    Managers & HR*. Eichinger, Lombardo & Ulrich.
    Lominger Limited, Inc., 2006.

3. Originated by Drs. Robert Kaplan (Harvard Business
    School) and David Norton as a performance measurement
    framework that adds strategic non-financial performance
    measures to traditional financial metrics to give managers
    and executives a more "balanced" view of organizational
    performance.

 **Chapter Three**

Sequence: The Linchpin of Organizational Effectiveness

Anything you build on a large scale or
with intense passion invites chaos.
—Francis Ford Coppola

The dilemma of 200 number one priorities

I joined Cisco Systems, Inc., (a leading internet hardware and infrastructure company) during one of its immense cycles of growth. Cisco had about 18,000 employees when I joined in November of 1999. When I was recruited away to BEA Systems in January of 2001 (about 15 months later), Cisco had grown to 43,000 employees. Needless to say, Cisco was experiencing growing pains. I remember its CEO, John Chambers, stating at an employee meeting that he was concerned that we, "might be losing the essence of who we are" with the ongoing rapid growth. At Cisco, I was hired to help develop the first consolidated software group, called Network Communications Software Group (NCSG), to be formed outside of the central OS team. It was unusual at that time for a hardware company to begin a push into software products and services, although a logical extension of Cisco's move toward an "end-to-end" product and services organization needed the software to support it.

During my first day on the job I was invited to a strategic planning session. The meeting room was heavy with tension and electricity. Seated around a U-shaped table were 16 executives, most of them former heads of acquired companies. Over the previous nine months Cisco had acquired 12 early-stage companies that had developed some aspect of network communications software necessary to drive its hardware solutions suite. I thought this move to be bold and challenging since Cisco was fundamentally a hardware company. Software groups find it difficult to survive in a predominately hardware environment and vice versa. I think this is due to a different approach, mindset, development cycle, etc., of the two disciplines—like mixing oil and water.

The meeting was being facilitated by two consultants from a boutique East Coast-based consulting firm. Bear in mind that this was my first day on the job with Cisco. One of my roles was to help design and implement the new organization for NCSG. Todd Murray, the senior executive, invited me to join the meeting as a way to meet the team that would drive this new entity. The task at hand was to literally prioritize the 193 projects (most of them underway) that had been aggregated from the executives of this newly forming organization. I had seen this situation many times before in other organizations.

Imagine this, a room full of highly intelligent, motivated executives, each making a business case for his or her agenda and the necessary headcount and resources required to implement that agenda. About 45 minutes into the meeting, Todd stopped the session because participants were beginning to show signs of frustration and conflict and said, "Allan, what do you think about this? Are we making good decisions about resource allocation?" My reply shocked the consultants and baffled the group. I said, "I think it's a moot point at this stage." Todd asked, "What do you mean?" I replied, "The initiative prioritization is out of context with the overall direction of the newly formed group. I know this because the vision and mission [shown on easel charts on wall] are not well-articulated. The mission hasn't been translated into imperatives [high-level objectives]. Also, we need to show the relationship between these 193 initiatives and the imperatives after sequencing the imperatives. Things are a bit backwards at this stage. So, it really doesn't matter how you prioritize the 193 initiatives right now since we are doing it out of context. It's a bit of a shot in the dark." The room was silent. One of consultants finally broke the silence, saying, "We can get these projects prioritized in about two hours. We've done this before with other clients and the process works well." Todd told the team to take a 15-minute break. He leaned over to me and said, "Okay, how do you suggest we proceed and please explain what you meant by 'sequencing'?"

> *"The sequence for building and operating an organization isn't necessarily apparent."*

I proceeded to explain to Todd that "if you're building a house, there's no argument about priorities; the focus is on determining or finding the right sequence in which to construct the house. There are many decision points along the way but the primary focus in on determining the most efficient order of the construction. For example, it is impossible to wire a house if the framing isn't in place first. You can't build walls until the foundation has been constructed. In a sense, building a house is a relatively simple undertaking when it comes to sequence because the inherent sequence is somewhat obvious." I continued, explaining to him that organizations, on the other hand, are complex because of the number of variables in motion. The sequence for building and operating an organization isn't necessarily apparent. In fact, it usually isn't obvious—you need to know how to find it. Sequence is a powerful concept in the efficient operation of organizations, which becomes apparent in practice. With so many activities simultaneously in motion (in a typical company), leaders gravitate toward "prioritization" (more likely on the functional level), which appears to be productive. But in reality, prioritization activities can become misleading and even diffuse resources—the opposite of what makes an efficient, robust organization. There is always an underlying sequence for work activity, but leaders need to know how to identify it. Planning algorithms always need to incorporate sequencing in the methodology. Once imperatives are identified and sequenced, much of the debate about priorities goes away. And when work activity (projects, initiatives, proposed programs) are vetted in a sequenced planning framework, these key learnings will occur: some projects will need to be deferred since these are too early in sequence; some initiatives will move up in queue; others will be stopped because these are irrelevant or too low in sequence to justify the effort and investment; and deltas or missing initiative work will be identified as being critical to some aspect of imperative completion. More than likely, these initiatives wouldn't have been discovered until major flaws in the plan or lack of company performance instigated a classic firefighting reaction.

"...prioritization activities can become misleading and even diffuse resources..."

Once the sequence is identified, I explained, then Todd's executive team would have a clear idea about the context of the playing field and what needs to be focused on in a relative order to achieve the mission. One doesn't need to get bogged down in a debate about priorities—an irrelevant activity at this stage—and a huge, ongoing time-synch for many leadership teams.

I told Todd, "We need to reset the planning effort. We're putting the cart before the horse. Let's review the mission, identify the key imperatives for NCSG, sequence these, then map the 193 initiatives [which were projected on the wall via PowerPoint] into the plan. Then we will be able to see what is important, what isn't, and what might be missing. The current discussion can't possibly reach a productive outcome for the company." Todd smiled, "Okay, you're on." I proceeded to facilitate the next day and a half of planning, much to the chagrin of the consultants, and helped NCSG create its first plan. Some 67 of the 193 original initiatives didn't make the cut in the sequenced plan and eight additional initiatives that weren't even on anyone's original list surfaced as mission-critical. I've always found this incredible. How could a room full of bright executives miss mission-critical work? Here's how: it gets lost in the complexity of a typical business environment, especially when a group consists of highly specialized functional experts not in the habit of or highly motivated to think cross-functionally.

Few organizations that I've worked with deploy resources in a sequenced manner. This is an especially dangerous dynamic for early-stage companies that are resource-poor. I've described "sequence" as the linchpin of organizational effectiveness because if leadership isn't operating and deploying resources in a sequenced manner then time and money is surely being wasted. With a focus on sequence, company leaders are not side-tracked into debates about what project or initiative is most important. During discussions, it's assumed that all initiatives are important. Sequence sets a planning team free from this Catch-22[1] and allows it to focus on identifying the critical path needed to build the house (the organization) in the most efficient manner. Note: a "critical path" is the sequence of stages determining the minimum time needed for an operation as defined by dictionary.com. A critical path, to be effective, should describe the efficient flow of initiative work (or project work), which is based on sequenced imperatives. Without the sequenced imperative infrastructure, the efficacy of the critical path is lacking.

Here's a little test to see if I've successfully implanted in your mind some new tracks of thinking. Which is a higher priority: 1) feeding the hungry, 2) reducing teen pregnancy, 3) balancing the state budget, or 4) protecting the environment? Any answer would be correct. These are all important topics and should be considered priorities. Thus, debating relative importance is not a productive activity. What *is* productive? Expend effort to create a strategic context (vision, mission, and imperatives), sequence the imperatives, and then address these topics in a sequenced plan. In doing so, we would quickly discover that many issues confronting us as citizens are symptoms of problems—and low in sequence (but no less important). By addressing more fundamental and foundational issues (like the foundation and walls of the house) we would be better-positioned to address other pressing and politically hot issues. As you might now deduce, many issues that appear high in priority turn out to be low in sequence. These issues can't be resolved until other, more foundational, matters are resolved. Given the lack of awareness on this topic, it's easy to see why many problems plaguing society seem to be difficult, if not impossible, to resolve.

Finding the sequence

In strategic planning, sequencing is a core activity that must be included in the creation of a Master Plan, discussed in Chapter Two. Leaders never want to get caught in the "prioritization debate," a low-value activity. It's critical that executives and practitioners alike understand how and when to use this methodology and know the difference between sequence and priority.

The tool I use for sequencing, called the Interrelationship Digraph and developed by Michael Brassard, was published during the quality movement of the 1980s. You can find a variety of Michael's tools in *The Memory Jogger Plus +²*, which has excellent coverage in support of planning activity.

During Mission Statement creation, it's most ideal to identify from 6 to 10 imperatives (high-level objectives). Too many imperatives mean that the planning work needs some additional refinement; too few imperatives are problematic—the thinking may be too compressed and generalized to translate adequately in the planning process. Next, the imperatives are sequenced using the Interrelationship Digraph, which provides a powerful, prescriptive framework in which to load and vet all initiative, program, and project activity.

The Interrelationship Digraph is a simple tool used to show the driver-and-result relationship between two activities (also known as the precursor and follower). We will use this tool to determine the sequential order of the imperatives. In Figure 3.1 below, I have listed two initiatives. Which is the driver (or precursor) and which is the result (or follower)?

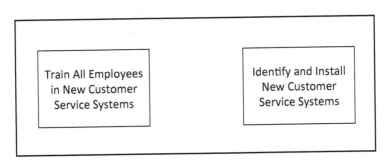

Figure 3.1: Two Initiatives in Search of a Sequence

In Figure 3.2, an arrow drawn between the two initiatives is used to show this relationship. In this situation, one would need to define the customer service system and make sure it was right for the company before investing in the training of employees. So, the arrow is drawn from the initiative that drives (or is precursor) to the initiative that is a result, or in this case, the follower: from "Identify and Install New Customer Service Systems" to "Train All Employees in New Customer Service Systems."

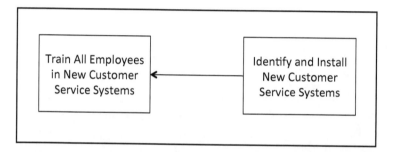

Figure 3.2: Finding the Sequence with an Interrelationship Digraph

The mechanics of the digraph are straightforward. Place your imperatives in a circle (preferably on yellow sticky notes that are then placed on an easel sheet) and draw arrows to identify the inherent sequence between them. Start with one imperative and then work your way around the circle asking, "What is the relation between the first imperative and the second? Which does the driving and which is the result (precursor, follower). Then draw an arrow from the driver to the result.

Let's develop the digraph by adding another imperative into the mix. With the addition of this new imperative, how does the digraph change? In the example below (Figure 3.3), I've worked my way around this small circle of imperatives drawing arrows to show the relation. It seemed to me that "Develop a Customer Service Strategy" was definitely the driver behind "Identify and Install New Customer Service Systems." I also felt that "Develop a Customer Service Strategy" needed to occur before "Train All Employees in New Customer Service Systems." With the arrows drawn, the digraph is scored to determine which imperatives are the key drivers and which are the results or followers in the sequence. Scoring is performed simply by counting the arrows out (drive) from an imperative noted on the left side of the equation and counting arrows in (follow) on the right side of the equation.

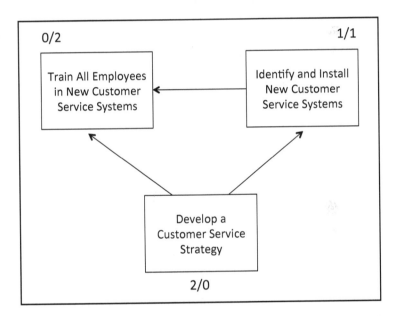

Figure 3.3: Finding the Sequence and Scoring the Digraph

In the upper-left corner, "Train All Employees in New Customer Service Systems" scored a 0/2 meaning that no driver arrows led out from the imperative and that two arrows led in. If you look at the scoring of the three headers you will immediately see that "Develop a Customer Service Strategy" is the clear driver, with a score of 2/0, whereas "Train

All Employees in New Customer Service Systems," with a score of 0/2, is being driven, or follows. The interpretation of this digraph is that a customer service strategy should be developed prior to identifying and creating systems or training employees. Note: All of these initiatives are important or of high priority. However, the sequence dictates that "Develop a Customer Service Strategy" is "foundational" and must be dealt with early in the work queue.

The interrelationship digraph becomes invaluable to finding the sequence in more complicated scenarios. For some imperatives there will be no obvious sequential relation with any of the others. While it's rare not to be able to identify a relationship, don't draw an arrow if you can't.

"...driver/precursor imperatives are the true enablers of the Master Plan."

Also, at times, it can be difficult to identify the sequential relationship between imperatives that haven't been fully defined by initiative work (the imperative is still vague). That's okay. While the process isn't an exact science, the underlying sequential imperative pattern will always surface. The completed interrelationship digraph will generate a sequencing outcome in which about one-third of the imperatives are drivers, or precursors; one-third results, or followers; and one-third somewhere in between. This doesn't mean that one imperative is more important than another. It does mean that driver/precursor imperatives are the true enablers of the Master Plan. Early progress here facilitates the achievement of the balance of the plan and sets the stage for effective resource utilization. The time-wasting, resource-sapping prioritization debate just became irrelevant.

Now let's take a look at two real-life examples of imperative sequencing and examine how this methodology can power up any planning process.

When I was working with Joe Weber, then the top executive at the Thermofit Division of Raychem Corporation, the planning objective was to improve the efficiency of his manufacturing division. After refreshing his mission statement, Joe's planning team determined that the following were the key divisional imperatives necessary to improve organizational effectiveness:

1. Use SPC on manufacturing process

2. Implement a suggestion system to get input from the line workers

3. Manage information exchange with our sister European operations more closely

4. Focus on measuring/reducing waste

5. Create global product specifications

6. Implement a comprehensive training program to include team building for all personnel

7. Create multifunctional work teams or cells to improve line-of-sight manufacturing

8. Promote a team-based culture with the necessary skills (which was lacking in the past)

9. Create a pay and progression system that was responsive to organizational and role changes

10. Implement a real-time information system

11. Add capacity planning skills, knowledge, and systems

12. Standardize and document processes; create and follow procedures

13. Implement a standardized planning process or algorithm

Prior to loading these imperatives into a Master Plan format we conducted a sequencing activity (using the Interrelationship Digraph) with Weber's top management team. Figure 3.4 is the outcome of that effort.

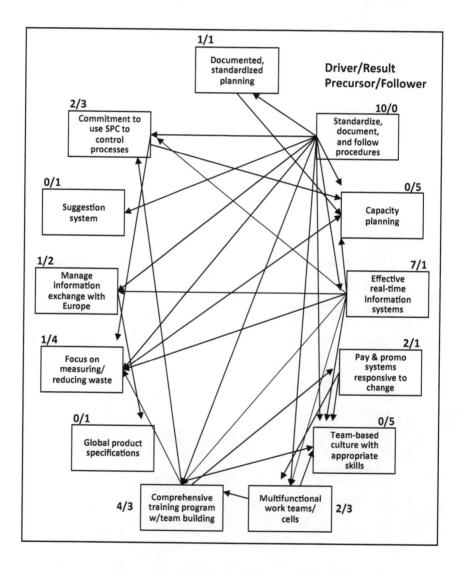

Figure 3.4: Raychem Thermofit Division
Manufacturing Imperative Sequencing

After completing and scoring the digraph, we learned this:

1. There were 3 primary drivers out of the 13 imperatives on the digraph. They were, in this order, Standardize and Document Processes, 10/0; Effective Real-Time Information Systems, 7/1; and Comprehensive Training Program with Team Building, 4/3.

2. Many imperatives had significant initiative and project work underway and yet several of these were not key drivers. Work was proceeding out of sequence. This was not apparent prior to this sequencing activity because of the complexity, large number of initiatives, and numerous management entities involved in executing the current fragmented plan.

3. Several initiatives related to these imperatives were corporate mandates, i.e., some of the initiatives were delegated from the office of the CEO. With this planning work, the stage was set to renegotiate the sequence in which imperatives and related initiative work was queued and completed.

In Chapter Two, "One Organization, One Blueprint," I used a former client, CTO Group, as an example in creating the Master Plan. I noted at that time that a crucial step for those involved was to sequence the imperatives once they were identified. Following is the sequencing work completed by the CTO Group (Figure 3.5, below). To reiterate, this organization was a newly created entity formed by merging an acquired datacom business with a telecom business. The Silicon Valley-based CTO Group served to provide a technical road map (context) for six global product lines (PLs) focused on inventing and building the next generation of wireless broadband equipment. While the actual data has been significantly edited here so as not to reveal the strategic content and any associated trade secrets and strategies, one can get a feel for how sequencing provides an important and necessary step in building a viable overall plan. The sequenced imperatives were then loaded into a Master Plan format and all ongoing and in-queue initiative work was also listed in the plan. Next, a leadership team vetting process occurred to determine the logical, sequenced (the order in which to build the house) resource deployment necessary to achieve the CTO Group's mission.

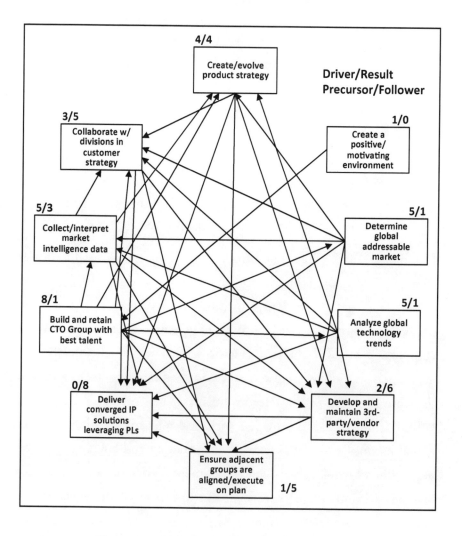

Figure 3.5: CTO Group Imperative Sequencing

I have had many entrepreneurs and company founders say to me, "This sequencing concept is just plain logic and we normally do this stuff in our heads." As I referenced in my opening remarks in this book, I think that company founders/entrepreneurs are some of the best innate planners. However, as organizations scale (more leaders, more geography, mixed cultures, and distributed decision making), the planning that occurs inside the head of the founder/entrepreneur becomes inadequate. Thus, tools like "sequencing" that help explicitly map the course of an organization and how resources will be deployed become crucial. This process, as with most of the others recommended in this book, helps create a transparent strategic planning algorithm that can unlock the mind power of many in the organization to create a common, aligned agenda.

I can't emphasize enough the importance of identifying the sequence when determining how a plan should be deployed. It is truly the linchpin (central cohesive element) of organizational effectiveness. Without it, available resources cannot be deployed in the most efficient manner. To many organizations, this can spell the difference between success and failure—achieving lift-off velocity and penetrating a market successfully or muddling through and missing key windows of opportunity. As stated earlier, a great idea doesn't mobilize itself. The yin needs the yang to achieve success.

Before I close this chapter I'd like to share another example of a planning format (Figure 3.6, below). This particular format, a Strategic Initiative Tree, was developed at BEA Systems as the company was in the process of plotting how to scale from $1 billion to $2 billion and beyond. On the chart, first the mission and related high-level goals were articulated; next, imperatives were identified; and then the extended executive team filled in the Strategic Initiative Tree to show what work needed to occur in order to achieve that multi-billion-dollar goal. The

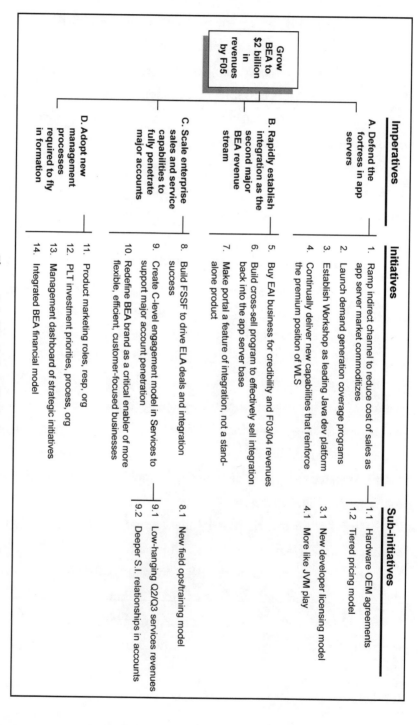

Figure 3.6: Strategic Initiative Tree

imperatives (only four are presented here) were too compressed at this stage for sequencing to be consequential. Sequencing then occurred at the functional level as each leader set his or her plan in motion. The functional plans were, of course, rolled up to the executive level and vetted appropriately as resources were allocated for the plan. This is not my preferred way to plot general imperatives, but it provides a quick way to map and understand the strategic landscape. This approach, if not used carefully, can underutilize vital information (e.g., Data Points) and give a false reading on actual work that needs to be performed. Note: this strategy-specific material regarding BEA Systems is being shared since the company no longer formally exists; it was purchased by Oracle, Inc., in 2008.

Chapter Three Notes

1. A Catch-22, coined and illustrated by Joseph Heller in his novel, *Catch-22*, is a logical paradox arising from a situation in which an individual needs something that can only be acquired by not being in that very situation; therefore, the acquisition of this thing becomes logically impossible.

2. *The Memory Jogger Plus+*. Michael Brassard. GOAL/QPC, 1989.

 Chapter Four

The Difference between a Team of Leaders and a Group of Leaders

Teams should be able to act with the same unity of purpose and focus as a well-motivated individual.

—Bill Gates

What keeps a venture capitalist awake at night? Well, for one, thinking such thoughts as "can the leadership team of the organization that I've just funded 'pull it off' and execute as a team?" VCs excel at scanning the market for opportunities (ideas) on which to bet their dollars. The huge unknown occurs when a $10-, $20-, or $30-million commitment is made to a start-up. Will the executive team be able to hang together through thick and thin and win (execute) as a team? The ability to do this goes far beyond having great talent. It was Jack Welch who said, in so many words, "The essence of competitiveness is liberated when we make people believe that what they think and do is important—and then get out of the way while they do it." Aphorisms like this make for great publicity and compelling literature. But, in reality, Welch was very successful as the CEO of GE by not just hiring great people but also organically (internally) growing great people. Welch didn't exactly practice what he preached. He created a dynamic playing field with specific rules and conditions for leaders, managers, and employees and managed relentlessly to that end: all of his leaders needed to perform assignments while operating in a very prescriptive GE culture. If his key talent and key leaders didn't perform well and play well with others—a precondition for being a leader in the GE culture, he was quick to act.

More often than not, the teaming ability at the top of the organization is the determinant of success or failure as opposed to the technology, product, or idea on which the company is based. The root cause of the flawed Hubble Telescope more than likely stemmed from team work rather than technology. Teaming or the lack thereof is what masked the problem. Scientists and engineers and subcontracting partners were not aligned and not working in the same context, which ultimately set them up for failure.

Teaming issues are endemic at the top

Literature that addresses the subject of teamwork is abundant and very old news. Generally, the programs for developing teams seem to be fairly straightforward, instructive in nature—and far from robust. Ironically, I have never consulted with an organization where the top executive team didn't need a "teaming" tuneup. Most were embroiled in a variety of issues that negatively impacted productivity and performance. The root cause? Key teaming elements were missing or needed improvement. This was the case whether the organization was pre-IPO or mature. I have been called in to help clients with strategy formulation, organization design, scaling methodologies, workforce planning, creating "Employer of Choice" cultures, location strategies, etc., yet in a significant number of instances the executive group demonstrated teaming traits that tended to be more problematic than the specific project or issue I was retained to resolve. In fact, I learned that if I didn't insist on addressing teaming issues upfront, the likelihood of project success (regardless of the assignment) not could, but would be compromised or even fail. Over time, with a little research and experimentation, I distilled the essence of "teaming" into a short instructional process that I will share with you here. I have used this as an essential first step in significant project undertakings and have always negotiated this precondition before accepting an assignment. It's made a world of difference in a company's effective operation. I should note that this process readily works in concert with the attention deficit syndrome that most executive teams appear to manifest in today's "just do it now" world.

Teaming issues seem endemic to executive-level teams. There are many reasons for this and the source of the problem suddenly occurred to me a few years ago in a most unusual setting. I was watching about 25 thoroughbred horses being herded into a ring (a circular corral about 100 feet in diameter). The horses began to run in a circle around the edge of the ring. Soon they were kicking and biting. After a while the horses were exhausted and calmed down a bit. Somewhat of a pecking order established itself but it was clear that not all of the horses wanted to be in this environment. Kicks and bites were still occasionally happening. I asked the attendant if what I had just witnessed was a regular occurrence. He replied, "Every time we put these high-strung thoroughbred animals in the ring together we get quite a show. It only happens with the thoroughbreds though. Put common horses together and there is much less commotion." I knew I had just witnessed an event similar to that which occurs in organizations when new executive teams are assembled and that this innate thoroughbred behavior that one sees in horses is very similar to what we see in our thoroughbred executives, leaders, and top talent. Thoroughbreds want to lead; they want to drive; they want to run on their own vector. Thoroughbreds don't naturally team well. It's not a good or bad thing—just the nature of the beast, so to speak. It takes a diligent upfront effort to instill and evolve teaming behavior; it won't naturally occur—or at least the leadership group will never fully evolve instinctively into a high-performing team. This is exactly what I've witnessed in numerous organizational settings: top teams (thoroughbreds) that begrudgingly get along and are civil to one another during formal meetings—but not much beyond that. Following formal meetings, the thoroughbreds run on their own respective courses.

> *"It takes a diligent upfront effort to instill and evolve teaming behavior..."*

This then raises an interesting question with regard to team effectiveness. How well can an organization perform if the top team's behavior is marginalized or to some degree dysfunctional? Like the conditions surrounding the flawed Hubble Telescope, not very. Even more problematic is when the top executives don't recognize team work as an issue. It's like a group of alcoholics trying to determine if they have a drinking problem. More than likely, they'll shift the problem to a beverage distribution issue or anything else not related to the root cause of alcohol addiction.

What is a team?

Two conditions must exist for a team to form: 1) a common goal or objective, and 2) one or more interdependencies. I like to use the "foxhole mentality" metaphor to describe this state: one person has the gun, one person has the bullets, and both are in a foxhole together being charged by an enemy. If either doesn't perform the assigned task, both die. Now that's a situation where teaming had better work and have undisputed objectives and interdependencies. It follows then that, if a leadership entity doesn't have common goals and objectives and clear interdependencies, then it is not a team. It is simply a group with the label of a team. Using titles such as C-level team, top team, executive team, and leadership team may sound great but it doesn't guarantee that, in fact, a high-performing team is functioning behind the name. So it is common to find many "executive teams" in reality performing more as "executive groups." There aren't clear interdependencies. Common goals and objectives may exist (or are certainly implied in the organization's purpose), but it's obvious to the casual observer that members of the executive group function fairly independently and in individual silos most of time—a loose federation of sorts.

Is teaming important?

One might ask, "What's the big deal? Maybe teaming at the executive level isn't that important. Many organizations work that way and still make piles of money." The only response I have to this kind of thinking is that it appears that, in fact, companies with high-performing teams generate more shareholder value and also demonstrate the ability to remain in business for many years. Jim Collins and Jerry Porras confirm this in their well-researched book, *Built to Last*[1].

Many very successful organizations have achieved lift-off velocity with a Draconian commander at the top. Is this the most productive and profitable model? Not likely. In fact, far from it. Michael Jordan, one of the best basketball players of all time said it very well, "Talent wins games, but teamwork and intelligence win championships." One of the best players to ever touch a basketball realized that he would need a high-performing team around him to win championships. His incredible talent alone could not get the job done. The sole purpose of teaming and related team building should be: 1) efficiency and effectiveness—to unlock the power of many minds focused and aligned on a topic, and 2) speed—to do things faster than an individual or a group could do it.

Team building is not a love fest

Teaming and team building is not about love, friendship, or warm fuzzies. Going there is where team-building activity got a bad rap and labeled as unnecessary. While bowling, ropes courses, and wine tasting can be great mixers and help socialize a group, those activities aren't team building—and do not contribute to the basic elements that need to be in place to achieve a high-performing team status. The reality is that groups of people with clear agreements about how they work together and with aligned expectations perform better than those that do not. Again, team building is about efficiency, effectiveness, and speed.

As I've noted above, executive team building is altogether a different situation because these groups tend to consist of many thoroughbreds. Executives deal with extreme demands, extreme stakeholder expectations, high-risk decisions, compressed time frames, and little room for error.

As with the thoroughbred analogy I've shared with you, whenever you put a group of smart, driven, innovative, and unusually successful people together in a confined space called an organization, expect running, kicking, and biting. This fact of nature and the reality of executive teaming must be acknowledged at the front end. So, team building for these groups (beyond common objectives and interdependencies) needs to include: 1) learning the nature of thoroughbreds, 2) developing signals or ways to notify one another that a bite or kick might be forthcoming, and 3) figuring out how to work through and manage this innate nature and minimize potential conflict and the turbulence that it creates in the work setting. As an example, when facilitating a strategic planning process with BEA Systems, I followed my own advice and conducted executive team building as a prerequisite with the extended executive team of about 23 participants. Following the team building we then reviewed work-to-date with regard to the strategy. During the session a brilliant technologist stood up and said, "I don't know what idiot wrote that strategy but we'll never grow the company on that path." This brilliant

> *"...team building is about efficiency, effectiveness, and speed."*

technologist (who now works for Google) in actuality knew that the top executive team, specifically the CEO, had created the strategy before he made his statement. Team building didn't modify this thoroughbred's behavior. We all know that it is difficult to change the nature of the beast. But the team-building process I had introduced had sensitized the executive team to the pros and cons (long-term damage) of this behavior and showed them how to manage through it when it would inevitably occur. Thus, this direct attack on the CEO did not become a show-stopper, killing the creativity and active idea exchange that was occurring in the room. All of a sudden the brilliant technologist became embarrassed by his behavior and realized that he was not contributing but rather sabotaging the progress of the team. The session continued with heated yet civil dialogue that showed the ability of this group of thoroughbreds to learn and rein in behaviors that, in the past, would have stopped the team from evolving (and melting down while in conflict).

Executives have to have thick skins. It's a prerequisite to occupy these top jobs. However, fighting words like "idiot" or "stupid" or comments veiled with a bit of levity like "they must have been smoking something when they thought this up" or "someone must have had a glass of wine when he wrote this" (all direct quotes from planning sessions) are what I term "fighting words." No one likes to be insulted, especially in a public setting. You can bet that even if a fighting word is used and no visceral reaction is witnessed in the meeting setting, one or more of the following delayed reactions will in fact occur: 1) retaliation happens at some point, 2) other team

"No one likes to be insulted, especially in a public setting."

members likely clam up for fear of a public attack like the one that just occurred and effectively shut down the creative process, and 3) strategic debate moves from an objective to an emotional level—where rational decisions and logic cannot prevail.

It's one thing to declare a group a team; it's another to commit to and invest appropriately to achieve that end point. But teams don't evolve without a concerted effort over time. A single team-building session or event can get things primed and going in the right direction—but is rarely adequate. It takes careful work and a deliberate evolutionary process in order for a group to evolve into a high-performing team. And, I should note that the technologist's bold comment above about a wrong direction or strategy proved to be right. The CEO had crafted a dead-end strategy—demonstrated by attending technologists later in the meeting. The good news is that the team-building process had prevented a meltdown (from thoroughbred behavior) and, the team continued to evolve the strategy until a workable blueprint had been crafted. Without the teaming foundation, that same session would have spiraled down into emotion and conflict—and certainly yielded a less-productive result.

Stages of team development

When we think "team" we need to realize that there are many kinds of teams. The rich variety of team types include: directed, self-directed, autonomous, conditional, self-managing, matrix, distributed, and virtual. All can be high- or low-performing. All have different types of mechanics and processes. My purpose here is not to explore the advantages and disadvantages of these different team types but rather to point out the similarities. Regardless of the team type, common goals, objectives, and interdependencies are required. After they're formed, all groups need to evolve through stages of team development. These stages cannot be skipped or jumped. Even if the team is loaded with experienced, highly educated executives, it must start at the beginning and mature through the stages—hopefully achieving high performance at some point. This doesn't occur without a deliberate effort to move from one phase to the next. It is a well-studied phenomenon. The good news is that team evolution can be accelerated by deliberately finessing its development through the phases.

In Figure 4.1 (below), I have superimposed three popular team evolution models [2]. I wanted to demonstrate the similarities of these evolutionary models that are found in the literature. Of the three models I prefer the one represented by the arrow: Forming, Storming, Norming, Performing by J.E. Jones. I find this model easiest to remember.

All teams begin as immature groups ("Forming"). A natural evolution begins: Who is who? Who is in charge? What's the agenda? How are we going to work together? When do we meet? How are we going to make decisions? This is very rudimentary and all teams must do it. What begins to occur next, like the thoroughbreds in the ring, is a bit more interesting. As a group is challenged with the pressures of determining the mission, objectives, allocation of resources, and identification of deliverables and decisions, these pressures move the group to the "Storming" stage. It is here that the thoroughbred dynamic will likely play out, especially with top teams. Teams can get stuck indefinitely at this stage because it takes awareness, energy, and knowledge to evolve through it. This is where formal team-building acumen becomes a competitive weapon for any leader.

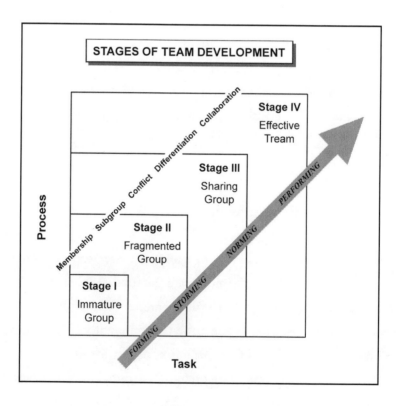

Figure 4.1: Stages of Team Development

What does it look like when a team is stuck in the "Storming" stage?

▷ Cliques and polarization can be seen among group members

▷ Some members avoid, blame, or act depressed whenever in the group environment

▷ It's clear that group members are defensive or even fearful; group dynamics are tense, extremely reserved, or strained

▷ Confrontational and antagonistic behavior can be seen in group dynamics

▷ Email is used as a forum for conversations that should be conducted face to face or used to resolve complex, difficult matters

▷ Group members use indiscreet forums to power up personal agendas or lobby for their respective viewpoints outside of normal team meetings

▷ Non-participatory behavior occurs

▷ Hierarchical behavior or "pulling rank" emerges when not necessary

▷ Diminished trust is seen

▷ Passive-aggressive behavior crops up

Most teams display at least some of these behaviors. It's human nature and certainly plays out when the team is made up largely of thoroughbreds. The trick is to acknowledge and head off these behaviors before they begin to bleed out into the organizational landscape—where they can severely compromise employee performance.

"Norming" is how a group breaks through and becomes worthy of the label of "team." "Norming" essentially determines the rules of engagement, how to manage inevitable friction, how decisions will be made, defining clear roles and responsibility and, of course, identifying common objectives and interdependencies. Even after a group begins to "norm" changes, such instances as a new member being added to the team can compromise the ability of the team to move forward. In this example, a new team member added in the "norming" phase needs to be afforded the opportunity to discuss, internalize, and buy in to elements that the team has already developed and agreed to. Until this is done, team evolution can't continue.

The final stage is "Perform" in which the team is now hitting its stride and has reached a state where maximum performance can be leveraged in the team setting. This is a nirvana state in terms of team work. If the integrity of the process has been maintained, the result can be a high-performing team: clear rules of engagement, minimal friction, decisions made and uniformly implemented, and, in the end, maybe a high-water mark for all team members. Note: as I mentioned earlier, team building and related team evolution is not about warm fuzzies and friendship. Team members don't need to love each other or love to work with one another. I think most people idealistically assume that this would be true in a "great team" setting. Not on the executive level. It can occur, but honestly I've seldom seen it happen. In fact if you try to build an executive team that is all about friendship (remember we're talking thoroughbreds here), then you're likely creating a rat's nest or "good old boy" atmosphere where decisions are based on relationships, friendships, conformance, and favors. This condition is the antimatter of effective teaming and a high-performing organization. I've worked with many large U.S. and foreign-based organizations and executive groups that are too steeped in their own cultures and circles of influence to ever get a glimpse of reality and the formula for a truly high-performing team.

As an example, I was working with Raychem Corporation back in

the late 1980's. A scientific-based company, Raychem had been successful for over 20 years in its market niches. Toward the end of Raychem's
reign I attended an all-employee meeting. The executive team was on
stage—12 white males, all from Ivy League schools and all between 45
and 65 years old. All but two had been with the organization for 20-
plus years. After the quarterly earnings presentation, the CEO began a
conversation about future growth and challenged all employees to improve themselves and help take the company to the next level. A woman
from the audience asked if he (the CEO) had considered improving the
diversity of the executive team as a
way to improve the company. The
CEO looked baffled and then said,
while waving his hand at the seated
executive team on stage behind
him: "I think we have tremendous

> *"When team building is underway, it's easy to get derailed by trying to make everyone friends."*

diversity. Bob went to Stanford, Clay to Cornell, Jim to Harvard, Harry
to Yale...[etc.]" The CEO was a serious and honest man. He was also
deeply embedded after graduate school in a culture that he had grown
up in. Not so ironically, the top team wasn't a team at all. It was a fraternity. The company managed that way for many years. This closed
"fraternity" culture grew and became successful, but, in the end it became
a liability. The gang of guys hadn't provided the top-team leadership
necessary to keep Raychem vital and able to climb the next Sigmoid
Curve. Raychem was acquired; the fraternity disbanded. It made me
wonder how far Raychem could have gone if it had been driven by a
high-performing team for all of those years. Maybe it would have become the next General Electric.

When team building is underway, it's easy to get derailed by trying
to make everyone friends. But it's not natural for everyone (especially

the thoroughbreds) to become friends. Endless socialization activities won't help. Focus on the core elements of building a great team. Those team members who don't become natural friends can carve out a civil working relationship, which can be productive and pleasant.

It takes work to evolve and maintain a high-performing team. The good news is that, if you are motivated to build a high-performing team, there's a good chance you can get there with the right process. The bad news is that teaming is easily sabotaged. White collar workers are incredibly talented at sabotage—intentional or not. In some respects teams are fragile because it takes only one member to turn things upside down and derail team work.

Here are a few examples of how one team member can undermine the team:

▷ Flaunt an altruistic attitude

▷ Multi-task during a team meeting

▷ Miss meetings

▷ Arrive late and/or leave early from meetings

▷ Be argumentative and use insulting language or humor

▷ Exhibit dominate behavior

▷ Talk but don't listen

▷ Not respond in a timely fashion to emails

▷ Be indecisive

▷ Engage in avoidance

▷ Hold side-bar conversations during a meeting

▷ Agree during a meeting but then take different actions outside the team setting

▷ Violate the confidentiality of team discussions

▷ Not participate in discussions

During team building sessions, I have asked executive teams to identify as many types of sabotage that they can remember witnessing in the work environment, which I would then list on an easel sheet. I've had to stop several groups after 30 minutes because we ran out of time and easel paper. The bottom line here is that it's easy to sabotage a team and undermine a team's effectiveness. And, it is extraordinarily easy for smart, educated executives to sabotage their own team, consciously or unconsciously. Team members must want to be team players and invest personally to help evolve team dynamics. The core elements needed to be in place for a team to form and continue to evolve as a team are:

1. Common goals and objectives and a process for keeping these objectives relevant, measurable, and monitored.

2. Clear interdependencies and a compensation system that reinforces interdependent behavior, i.e., there are no winners on a losing team.

3. Team Agreements or Rules of Engagement: rules for the thoroughbreds to play by and govern key behavior, i.e., how to manage friction, how to hold one another accountable, how to have constructive debate, how to build trust and the necessary degree of working compatibility.

4. Clear team expectations and processes: when to meet, how to communicate, how decisions will be made.

5. Thorough education so that all team members understand the normal evolutionary stages, what gets in the way of this evolution, and how to minimize both purposeful and accidental sabotage.

6. A periodic team work assessment, or what I call a "Team Alignment Check" to keep team dynamics alive and continuously improving.

Before I close this chapter I would like to share four key tools, a couple mentioned above, that I have found to be most helpful in developing high-performing teams: Rules of Engagement, Team Agreement Alignment Check, Individual Commitment, and Decision Matrix.

Team Agreements, or Rules of Engagement

A pivotal activity needed to help groups evolve into teams is creating Team Agreements or Rules of Engagement. Have team members identify the 6 to 10 necessary characteristics or traits that they believe their team needs to exhibit in order to work together effectively. There is a subtle difference in these characteristics from team to team. What really matters is that a newly forming team invest the time necessary to identify, debate, and internalize these traits and then make every effort to behave this way. The importance of the discussion and process is to sensitize team members to these traits—what these traits look like and feel like when performed correctly or incorrectly. This doesn't guarantee that executive behavior will immediately conform. It does, however, give the team awareness and license to begin holding one another accountable (in a productive manner)—a key trait of a high-performing team. If Team Agreements are left to chance and not formally declared, there is a higher likelihood that instances of sabotage—intentional or unintentional—will surface. I believe that a paramount activity and responsibility of any leader is to ensure that the top team is working together as productively as possible. Any teaming missteps or misalignments that occur at the executive level have an exponential impact (rippling effect) on the overall organization.

Below are the Team Agreements crafted by the former BEA Systems Operations Management Team (an extended executive team of 18 leaders) and the CTO Group at Redback Networks. Prior to one of the sessions at which these agreements were created, I remember riding up in the elevator with one of the executive-level technologists. He said, "We're doing team building this morning?" I replied, "Yes." He said, "I've done this activity in five other companies. It's a waste of time." I replied, "Are those companies still in business?" He turned his back on me and exited the elevator. After the three-hour session, this same executive invited me to perform a similar team building activity with his executive team. I bring this up not to blow my own horn but to bring home the point that he got the message. What had likely impressed him was that we addressed the core of "team evolution" in the session, not socialization activities. He saw the benefits and potential productivity gains to be had with this approach.

> *"A pivotal activity needed to help groups evolve into teams is creating Team Agreements."*

When helping BEA Systems create its Rules of Engagement, I asked the executive team to consider these questions:

1. Think about the characteristics of great teams that you have been a part of in the past. List those characteristics that promoted success.

2. Given what you know today (with regard to business context, the current group dynamics, job demands, etc.), what are the key agreements that you think are most important for this team to observe (govern team dynamics) in order to be wildly successful?

3. For each team agreement determine how team members can help each other with mutual accountability, i.e., if the team or member of the team is not following the agreement, how is this situation constructively handled?

Here is a sampling from the Team Agreements generated during BEA Systems' OMT session. These agreements were the work of a group of thoroughbreds that had struggled previously to work effectively together. Note that each agreement lists an accountability. I have found that it is helpful to have the newly forming team specifically note how members of the team will hold one another answerable to the team commitments. Getting each team member in the act of keeping the team agreements alive and well is a great way to ensure that the agreements in fact come to life. Otherwise, the team leader will wind up trying to police commitments—which derails progress toward a high-performing team state.

▷ As a team, define roles and responsibilities in the context of agreed-to objectives. Do this activity whenever new objectives surface. *Accountability: the management team is responsible for identifying and agreeing to objectives, defining roles and responsibilities, and executing against these with periodic validation.*

▷ Be tolerant of one another, but don't tolerate emotionally based behaviors that attack a person. "Attack the point, not the person." *Accountability: positive confrontation.*

▷ Commit to communication and follow-through—no dropping the ball. *Accountability: call each other on "ball-dropping" without negative, emotionally based behaviors.*

▷ Be prepared. Be a value-added member of the team. *Accountability: if not ready, don't go; if a commitment can't be kept, inform the team ahead of time.*

Here is an example of Team Agreements crafted by Redback Networks' CTO Group. This was a newly forming team in an environment where technologists had historically been working in silos. While the agreements may seem like a "non event," in reality these were huge steps for the group to take toward working as a team:

> ▷ Work toward a shared vision and a common set of objectives. *Accountability: periodically review the company and CTO group mission and objectives and test for alignment.*

> ▷ Support an environment where you can earn trust and respect. *Accountability: assume team members will deliver on commitments and hold one another accountable.*

> ▷ Create an environment where we can openly challenge activities and initiatives to ensure that these are aligned with the overall vision and objectives. *Accountability: be open to reprioritize and adjust our activities as required.*

> ▷ Leverage innovative and productivity-enhancing tools where practical. *Accountability: discuss a plan of action and agree on it as a team.*

Again, Team Agreements might not seem too important to some—especially in the executive ranks. I think it is easy to become enamored with or caught up in our products, technologies, and services and forget that the machinery on which organizations run is behaviorally based. Without people, organizations don't exist. Once the Team Agreements are created, I print these on a form and have all team members sign theirs—a contract of sorts. Then a short celebration is held. The group has now evolved to the "Norming" stage—and moved closer to becoming a high-performing team. I also frame these agreements and send them out to each team member to help reinforce that this is the code by which this team will behave going forward.

Alignment Check to keep the thoroughbreds productive

It's not enough to simply create Team Agreements. To accelerate and maintain the evolution of a team, one must periodically (at least three to four times a year) invest a bit of time to refine the agreements, test for alignment, and make any necessary adjustments. For this purpose, I created a simple, quick, visual tool to examine team alignment (Figure 4.2 below). At these Alignment Check meetings, I enlarge this simple format to easel size, insert the Team Agreements and then have all team members periodically place sticky-dots on the model. Aligned agreements are within the arrow and misaligned agreements are to the left of the arrow, in columns that show the degrees of misalignment (1, 2, or 3, with "3" indicating great misalignment). Here is an example of an Alignment Check, prepared by the international controller's team at SAP, Inc., and the respective alignment pattern:

I then have the team analyze the pattern and chose two or three key misalignments to work on between this session and the next pulse check. This activity keeps teaming in the forefront and helps promote open dialogue (in a constructive manner) with regard to teaming issues. Thoroughbreds need this more than the average team and will likely resist the effort, but as discussed earlier, this is where the game of "organizational effectiveness" is won or lost.

Individual Commitments

In addition to the Team Agreement Alignment Check, I always have team members conclude the activity by writing down "Individual Commitments" or what each team member will personally do between now and the next meeting to help address any misalignments. I have found that this activity helps drive individual ownership—and puts team members on the hook to make change. Team members list just one or two personal actions and then we review these as a group. I collect the Individual Commitments, make copies, send them back out and, yes, start the next session reviewing progress on the Individual Commitments. This is quite successful in facilitating incremental behavior change in executive ranks.

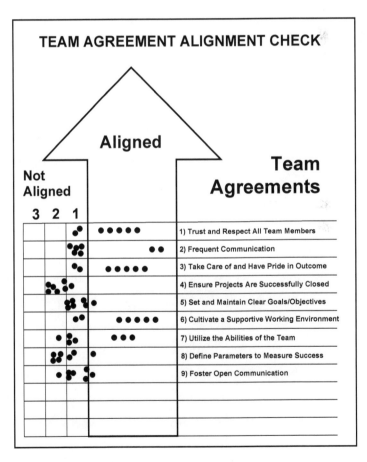

Figure 4.2: Team Agreement Alignment Check

The Decision Matrix

Decision making the old "hierarchical" way usually doesn't work in modern-day organizations. There are many reasons for this: the span of control is too great, the speed of the business too fast, geographies and cultures too complex, etc., for simple hierarchical decision making to work. There are multiple stakeholders who usually need to be involved in the decision making process, consulted with, informed, and so on, in order for decisions to be followed and to stick. To facilitate effective decision making, I use a Decision Matrix as a vetting agent to address most of the common decisions that surface in the team setting. In the matrix (Figure 4.3, below), one simply inserts the typical/routine decisions that are made, lists the stakeholders that need to be considered in the decision process, and then works through the decisions, one at a time, using the CAIRO model. CAIRO stands for Consult, Approve, Inform, Responsible, and non sequitur or not applicable ("O"). This isn't just a one-time activity; the matrix helps jump-start and even head off potential collisions that occur on the executive level. You can bet that this activity will force clarification of roles and responsibility, identifying who and where the stakeholders are, and proactively addressing differences embedded in the organizational structure. It is a worthwhile time investment—one that further accelerates the maturing of a team and its awareness of the dynamic stakeholder environment surrounding it.

Team development is essentially a free activity. An organization doesn't need to spend a lot of money to create and evolve high-performing teams. What's most critical is that a top executive team realize that, first and foremost, it must operate effectively—and demonstrate this to the balance of the organization. No one is fooled when a top team isn't working well together. In some instances it becomes even laughable to the organization at large. The emperor wears no clothes. Team building is the base camp for building a high-performance corporation. Very related to this discussion and the topic is Chapter Five, "The CEO Killer: Misunderstood and Mismanaged Stakeholders." Effective teaming includes explicit connections with the large web of stakeholders that exists in any organizational setting.

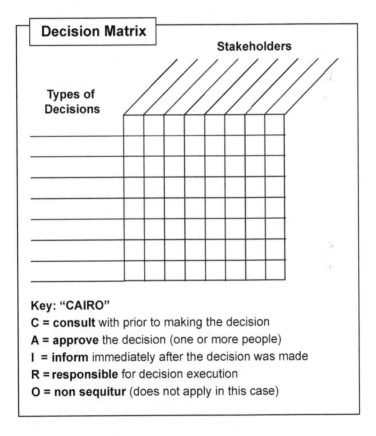

Figure 4.3: Decision Matrix

In closing this chapter I will leave you with a memorable image. A cartoon strip I recently saw in the newspaper showed two astronauts walking across a lunar surface back to their command module. The inscription read, "No reason to be here any longer, there's nothing to kill." As we have discussed, the nature of the thoroughbred is to be energetic and aggressive in spirit, performance, and intention. This innate behavior can be channeled for the benefit of the organization or left to manifest itself in ways that can become unimaginably deadly to the health of that same organization. An effective team of leaders at the top of the company can tip the scale from underachievement to wildly successful. Just remember, as civilized as we might think we are, we carry a slew of less-desirable behaviors in our DNA—which can surface at any time and derail progress. It's up to us to proactively manage this proclivity.

Chapter Four Notes

1. *Built to Last.* Collins & Porras. HarperBusiness, 2004.

2. Membership, Subgroup, Conflict, Differentiation, Collaboration – David Bradford & Allan Cohen, 1997; Immature Group, Fragmented Group, Sharing Group, Effective Team – J.E. Jones, 1973; Forming, Storming, Norming, Performing – Bruce Tuckman, 1965

Chapter Five

The CEO Killer: Misunderstood and Mismanaged Stakeholders

*Most discussions of decision making assume that only senior
executives make decisions or that only senior executives'
decisions matter. This is a dangerous mistake.*
—Peter Drucker

Unless you are working alone in a cave carving hieroglyphics on the
wall, you have stakeholders. It stands to reason that larger organizations have larger stakeholder slates to manage. Note that I used the word
"manage" here and this is the focus of this chapter. If, as an executive or
leader or someone with responsibility, you are not actively managing the
stakeholders in your sphere of influence, then your longevity in your role
is at risk. Yes, your job is at risk even if you are doing exactly what the
organization needs and wants you to do.

What's a stakeholder?

The term, "stakeholder," was first used in a 1963 internal memo at the
Stanford Research Institute. It defined stakeholders as "those groups

without whose support the organization would cease to exist." This definition has evolved over the years to mean "someone, a group, or entity that has an interest in a deliverable or outcome." This can be expanded to state: "A person, group, or organization that has a direct or indirect stake in an organization because it can affect or be affected by the organization's actions, objectives, and policies."[1] Stakeholders in a business include, for example, customers, directors, employees, agencies, owners (shareholders), suppliers, unions, creditors, and the community from which the business draws its resources.

I was conducting a strategic planning effort for a client, and when we reached the topic of "stakeholder management," I was hit with an emotional reaction from the ranking executive: "I don't have time to figure out and do all of this stakeholder management stuff. I've got a business to run." Two months later David Smith (last name changed to protect his identity) was removed from his job as senior vice president of the products division (about 2,300 employees and $700 million in revenue).

I wasn't able to convince David to invest time in stakeholder management. Had we engaged in this activity maybe David would still be in his job today. Here's a bit of history to fill in the blanks of this story.

The power and influence of stakeholders

David was a visionary and a technical genius. I had worked with him several years prior to the above incident when he was an emerging top talent in the organization, a Fortune 500 global manufacturing company. He had recently been promoted to the group level and given the title of SVP to run a troubled products division. The division had a revolving door at the top. (This should be a red flag to any incoming executive that stakeholders' agendas are not aligned and running amuck.) Four leaders had occupied the top job in as many years. Productivity was poor. Employee turnover was above industry rates. The product road map wasn't clear and was a topic of constant debate in the executive ranks. Current products had feature and quality issues. Several key customers were threatening to jump to the competition if long-standing quality issues weren't resolved.

Now David enters the picture. Here is a bright guy, an innovator, a driver personality with a touch of altruism—typical of many leaders—thinking that he can jump in with immediate credibility, save the day and turn this division into a showcase for the company.

After working with David to revise the strategy, product road map, and organization design, I was certainly convinced that he had formulated a solid, defensible plan. It was likely the right path to get this division on its

> *"Powerful stakeholder groups organically form—and these groups are keenly interested in outcomes that serve their respective agendas."*

feet and performing. The work included stakeholder identification and it was clear that there were significant stakeholder issues that needed managing. But David dug in and refused to invest additional time on this activity. He believed that actions spoke louder than words. "Let them (the stakeholders) judge me by my results," he declared. David believed that he could address any outstanding stakeholder issues through the normal scheduled meetings that plastered his calendar. In the end, he never got a chance to implement his plan. In the scheme of things, his strategy was moot and it didn't even matter if his plan was the best possible course of action for the company. This is one of the mindless aspects of these large social systems that we call organizations. Powerful stakeholder groups organically form—and these groups are keenly interested in outcomes that serve their respective agendas. If stakeholders don't believe that the leader is executing a plan that serves their specific purpose (and you can bet stakeholder have limited and sometimes distorted views of what's really going on behind the scenes), then plan implementation can get derailed.

As I mentioned in a previous chapter, it's not enough to have great products, services, and/or technology. Pure innovation doesn't stand alone well in today's fast, complex organizational settings. In David's case, he had stepped into a stakeholder quagmire. This environment had a history of gobbling up executives—or at least the ones who couldn't recognize the complex idiosyncrasies of the stakeholder environment and proactively manage it. Herein lies the lesson: effective stakeholder management is a critical, non-negotiable element in running an organization.

Stakeholder power is increasing

What's worse is that stakeholders today have more influence over an organization than in the past. Stakeholders also have a higher degree of sophistication, education, and expectation that, if left unmanaged, might lead to unfortunate consequences. I recently worked for a German-based software giant named SAP. Its structural environment had a minimum of five hierarchical dimensions layered into its global matrix organization. This was "stakeholder central." A typical senior executive had at least two bosses and sometimes three or four. Many times, adjacent organizations within SAP had more power and influence over a division's agenda than the normal hierarchy. In meetings during which I'd try and help identify the stakeholder landscape, I'd run out of time and energy trying to map the layers of stakeholders for a given business unit.

Do we really need to design organizations that are this complex to navigate? And, if you sign up to lead in these kinds of environments, is it not critical to be prepared to make a sizeable investment in stakeholder management—certainly not the first passion for many innovators, leaders, and technologists? Imagine the amount of time and energy that is required on the part of a leader to navigate this kind of organization! And productivity? Out the window.

Net–net, if you want to be a successful executive and/or leader it's absolutely essential that you: 1) identify your stakeholders, 2) understand stakeholder needs, ex-

> *"...stakeholders today have more influence over an organization than in the past."*

pectations, and current perceptions, and 3) proactively manage these stakeholders' perceptions. If you don't, yours may be the next CEO obituary in *The Wall Street Journal*.

In 1999 Hewlett-Packard named Carly Fiorina its chief executive officer, succeeding Lewis Platt. Carly was brought in from the outside securing the job over an internal incumbent. She was the first woman to lead a Fortune 20 company. Carly was terminated by the board of directors in 2005. There has been a lot of debate since over the strategic direction that Carly took HP. There was the acquisition of EDS and Compaq and the repositioning of many of HP ventures. However, after speaking with a number of insiders (current and former HP executives), analysts, and CEOs of HP's direct competitors, I deduced that it was Carly's stakeholder management, not her strategy, which led to her downfall. Carly seemed content to be aloof to employees (HP's long-standing culture is "management by walking around" with egalitarian overtones), was at odds with key board members and investors over company direction, and maintained a loosely federated executive team that demonstrated a lot of infighting and politicking. Need I go further? I suspect that Carly was an adequate strategist. Mark Hurd, her successor, appeared to implement Carly's strategy verbatim with a bit of Draconian cost-cutting added for good measure.

We'll never know if Carly could have taken HP to a new plateau of success. What I suspect is that she was inadequate in her ability to identify and manage stakeholder expectation in support of her agenda. Many missionaries have been killed and eaten by natives who didn't believe and weren't willing to follow. It's no different in the corporate world.

In my files, I have nearly 20 examples of recent situations that I can cite where stakeholder management, or the lack thereof, created an untenable situation for a leader. In most cases, the executive was ejected from the organization or, at minimum, put in the penalty box (moved to a non-consequential role). As an example, Carol Bartz was recently publicly beheaded (fired) as CEO of Yahoo, Inc. On her exit she called Yahoo board members "doofuses." I'm not saying that poor leadership, poor strategies, poor performance, and the like couldn't have been factors in this and other dismissals. What I am saying is that stakeholder management must be included in a successful leader's plan and her executive team must also be sensitized to help manage the stakeholder landscape.

The emperor has no clothes

This brief paragraph is a personal note from me to all of those leaders, innovators, and executives out there running companies. Having worked with hundreds of such individuals, I can state with certainty that the key ingredient in people's DNA that enables them to rise to the top and lead organizations with power, money, influence, and authority can also be a curse. The ability to be wildly successful carries with it a blind spot or the inability to understand the limits of that influence, power, and authority. Why else would so many smart, talented, driven individuals with phenomenal career tracks flame out, making obvious mistakes and even breaking conventional rules and norms that lead them to ruin. Who in their right mind would ignore or purposely incite stakeholder groups? While effective stakeholder management will not stop a leader from breaking the law or performing Darwinian acts of self-destruction, it will certainly head off 95% of the key problems inherent in running any complex organization loaded with special interest groups—and will give that same executive the best possible chance of successfully executing on her agenda.

How to identify and manage the stakeholder landscape

All stakeholders are not equal and different stakeholders or stakeholder groups require different levels of consideration. In this light I have devised a very simple, straightforward method to ensure that stakeholders are identified and managed and that related actions are incorporated into the plan. There are no hard and fast rules here. What is important is that time is invested in identifying, evaluating, and determining those actions needed to gain endorsement and support from key stakeholder entities.

I advise executives and leaders to examine stakeholders on two levels: 1) Impact: what influence does this stakeholder have on my ability to get things done and achieve success? and 2) Perceived Status: is the stakeholder supportive of my plan and progress to date?

Stakeholder Impact is separated into three categories: 1) A sponsor or someone or some group that needs to endorse my agenda (rated "A"). Without it I can't proceed. Sponsors might have final approval of budgets and/or headcount and hire/fire power over the leader performing the stakeholder analysis. There should be only a few stakeholders with an "A" rating, 2) Individuals or groups that need to buy in, commit to, or, at a minimum, support the agenda (rated "B"). Without their help on some level, it will be difficult to achieve success, and 3) Individuals or groups with whom it's politically correct and important to include in the information loop and keep up to date (rated "C"). These stakeholders exert indirect influence that may or may not have immediate consequences.

"Including [stakeholders] in this process helps eliminate surprises and facilitate the agenda..."

What is important here is to recognize that these stakeholders do exist and may have underestimated power over a leader's agenda and related actions. Including them in this process helps eliminate surprises and facilitate the agenda; exclusion can undermine it.

The Perceived Status rating is your best guess (or the leadership team's, if performing this activity as a group) as to whether or not the stakeholder is in fact supporting your agenda (i.e., positive), indifferent or unsure about your agenda (neutral), or directly or indirectly hindering the achievement of the agenda (negative).

In rating each stakeholder individual or entity on Impact and Perceived Status, you have the making of a working document that can be managed over time. I tell all clients that a stakeholder with an Impact rating of "A" or "B" coupled with a Perceived Status rating of "neutral" to "negative" is a red flag. Many such ratings on the stakeholder slate are an indication that it will be extremely difficult to implement intended actions. After having clients perform the Stakeholder Analysis, I've had many of them recognize that it may be impossible to be successful in the environment and/or that the path forward will require too many compromises—leading to an undesirable result. Don Smith (named changed to mask identity), the fifth head of engineering for Redback Networks in seven years, left the company after six months on the job. Redback Networks had been purchased by Ericsson, Inc., a global Swedish-based telecommunications company. His reason for leaving? After identifying and meeting with key stakeholders, he didn't believe that he could implement the necessary engineering agenda to achieve success. The Redback/Ericsson stakeholder landscape was too complex and had conflicting expectations about what constituted a successful engineering agenda. After resigning, Don went back to Cisco Systems where he knew the stakeholder environment would be supportive of his ideas and methods. Don said he left Redback because the environment there had too many powerful stakeholders with very different ideologies and views about the technical road map. "I didn't think I could be successful there—and it wouldn't have been fun trying." To me, this was a sign of an astute executive. He was able to read the stakeholder environment and make proactive choices. As an aside, eventually Ericsson brought in a long-term Ericsson head of engineering from another division. Three years later this leader is still trying to figure out how to organize and drive a successful Silicon Valley-based engineering organization.

Here are two examples (significantly abridged to protect identities) of the stakeholder management process. The first analysis was completed by an incoming CEO of a medium-sized business; the second was completed by a divisional CTO at a Fortune 500 company.

Stakeholder management—example one

The first example, (Figure 5.1, below), is work performed by a new CEO in the process of establishing herself with an existing organization and executive team. No internal incumbent had been chosen for the CEO position and two internal C-level executives felt that they should have been chosen: the chief technical officer and the chief sales officer. The board of directors asked the incoming CEO to make every effort to keep the existing executive team intact and make it work, having removed the former CEO for poor company performance. This is a global hi-tech organization with 2,500 employees operating in 21 countries. The CEO listed all of those organizations/entities and related stakeholders she deemed crucial at the time of the analysis. Note: a stakeholder can be an individual or a group, e.g., employees are a stakeholder group, and the board of directors is a stakeholder entity or group, however, one might call out (identify in the plan) individual stakeholders who are members of the board if they have extraordinary influence and power that needs specific attention.

Organization/ Entity	Stakeholder	Impact	Perceived Status	Owner	Action Steps
BOD		B	Neutral	CEO	Meet 1:1; Buy-in during strategy devel.
	Tom W.	A	Positive	CEO	Weekly 1:1 to keep in sync
	Bob S.	A	Neutral	CEO	Meet 1:1. Devel. rapport & expectations
	Martha G.	B	Negative	CEO	Meet 1:1. Devel. rapport & expectations
Partners	Magnus A.	B	Positive	CSO	Meet to refine agreements
	John S.	C	Neutral	CEO	Devel. relationship & refine agreements
Investors	Bob L.	B	Positive	CEO	1:1/Meet with Bob during Sandhill trips
	Mark W.	C	Neutral	CTO	Give Ken (CTO) relationship assignment
Analysts	Debra M.	C	Neutral	CEO	Discussion strategy 1:1
	Kevin B.	C	Negative	CFO	Discuss strategy & relationship build
Exec. Team		B	Neutral	CEO	Devel. informal time & clear expectations
CTO	Ken B.	B	Negative	CEO	1:1 to gain support & set expectations
CSO	Luther D.	B	Negative	CEO	1:1 to gain support & set expectations
Engineering	David S.	B	Neutral	CTO	1:1 to gain support & set expectations
Employees		B	Neutral	Exec. Team	Communicate compelling vision, brand, & upside for careers & earnings
Management		B	Positive	Exec. Team	Clarify strategy; implement monthly all-managers meeting for branding/alignment
Customers		B	Neutral	Exec. Team	Create/enact customer coverage plan
DBL	Robert T.	B	Neutral	CEO	1:1 to gain support & refine action plan
ETSC	Mary M.	C	Positive	CSO	Ask Mary for branding support
SIRA	Huang W.	C	Negative	CSO	1:1 to gain support & refine action plan

Figure 5.1: Stakeholder Analysis—Example One

This abridged version of a stakeholder management plan was created with the new incoming CEO and the advocate board member who helped facilitate her hire (Tom W. on the chart). The results of the analysis were concerning. Some 15 of the 20 Perceived Status ratings were neutral to negative. Only five were positive. This new CEO had a huge amount of work to do to manage stakeholder perception. This meant countless one-on-one meetings to build relationships; overcoming negative views based on history, strategy, and company performance; and a willingness to commit to relentless communication to manage perception.

Great executives do this unconsciously. Some executives, especially those with a deep technical or scientific orientation, tend to stumble when it comes to stakeholder management. Regardless of one's capability, I would suggest that it is critically important to perform the stakeholder analysis in writing for three reasons: 1) the stakeholder analysis becomes a formal Data

> *"Stakeholder management is the ultimate enabler for an executive's agenda."*

Point and part of the plan (to be reviewed, revised, and constantly worked like any other initiative), 2) portions of the written document can be delegated to other executives so that stakeholder management tasks can be shared, and 3) that which is measured, in corporate settings, usually gets managed. This task can't be left to chance. Stakeholder management needs to be a built-in planning algorithm. If performed well, then everything from strategy buy-in to approvals for funding and employee support are easier to facilitate. When managed correctly the stakeholder environment works in support of an executive's agenda, rather than against it. Surprises on either side of the equation are minimized. Stakeholder management is the ultimate enabler for an executive's agenda.

Stakeholder management—example two

In my second example (Figure 5.2 below), a newly appointed divisional CTO and his new team had struggled to get the engineering organization and adjacent divisions to agree to and implement their product road map. After eight months of effort with little progress, a stakeholder analysis was performed as part of a strategic planning effort. You'll note that this is a typical large-scale company environment that has an abundance of internal stakeholders within the same division or adjacent divisions. This is the classic matrix organization—advanced citizenship is required here to deal with all of the groups, entities, individuals, processes, policies, and the like.

Each division had a president and CTO (and other C-level staff), plus product line groups that designed and then built the respective hardware and software. The role of the divisional CTO was to create a "technical road map" so that all product line groups had a plan to follow. Disagreement and conflict was occurring between the CTO group and the product line groups—and other divisional counterparts that were either threatened by the CTO agenda or simply not willing to support his technical road map. This CTO had a history of being one of those visionary technical innovators (but who had never navigated an environment with this complexity). I explained to him that it didn't matter if his technical vision was correct (correct, of course, helps), but what did matter was his ability to socialize and gain support for his technical vision in this extremely complex stakeholder environment. Also, many of the stakeholders were less threatened by the technical vision and more obstructionist because he—an outsider to the culture—was challenging the status quo. So, the stakeholder management activity here was paramount. If he couldn't generate some degree of stakeholder support, then the technical agenda that his team had crafted was dead on arrival.

Organization /Entity	Stakeholder	Impact	Perceived Status	Owner	Action Steps
Product Lines					
PL One	Shai A.	B	Positive	CTO	Maintain relationship & support
PL Two	Alisa T.	B	Neutral	Alfredo V.	Share technical road map & gain buy-in
PL Three	Jason W.	B	Negative	Mark C.	Meet & determine a way forward
PL Four	Mark Y.	B	Negative	CTO	Meet & determine a way forward
Corp Groups					
Prod Mgmt	Melissa E.	B	Neutral	Jan G.	Create a relationship & periodic contact
Sales Mgmt	Magnus L.	C	Negative	CTO	Share agenda & gain support
Marketing	Luke C.	C	Neutral	Ian W.	Share agenda & gain support
Global Biz Mtg	Ranie S.	C	Positive	Jan G.	Maintain relationship; invite to off-site
Div Groups					
Tech Sales Sup	Mark W.	B	Positive	CTO	No additional actions at this time
Mktg/Comm	Jane T.	C	Positive	Ian W.	Maintain relationship
Engineering	Prassad V.	B	Neutral	Justin M.	Share technical road map/next steps?
Biz Devel	David F.	C	Neutral	Ian W.	Hold summit to agree on agenda
Div President	Carl I.	A	Positive	CTO	Share stakeholder analysis/gain support
Div Sales	Brian M.	C	Positive	CTO	No additional actions at this time
Customers					
KBT	Kevin B.	C	Negative	CTO	Invite Kevin to in-house tech demo
China ML	Jonny H.	B	Neutral	CTO	Delegation to ML – road show
URX	Ernest V.	C	Positive	Alfredo V.	Continue with beta; periodic check-ins
TQMS	Stephan S.	C	Positive	Mark C.	Gain buy-in to perform beta & road show
DSIN	Johan T.	B	Neutral	CTO	Delegation to DSIN – road show

Figure 5.2: Stakeholder Analysis—Example Two

In the example above, the CTO worked with his respective team to perform the Stakeholder Analysis. Some 11 of the 19 stakeholders in this initial analysis carried a neutral or negative rating, so, there was certainly work to do to shift this environment from one that would block or disable the CTO group agenda to one that would support it. The team of technologists also was aghast by the effort needed to manage stakeholder perception and initially resisted the activity. After completion, all parties recognized the stakeholder patterns in the company's environment that blocked their ability to be successful. One technologist stated, "I'm a technologist, not a politician…but I can see that one can't survive without the other in this environment."

Like it or not, that statement holds true in most environments.

What if I dislike a stakeholder, disagree with a stakeholder's agenda, and/or the stakeholder won't work with me? These are common concerns. As noted in the team building section, you don't need to like the people you work with. It certainly helps, but it's not a prerequisite. In this case it's important to figure out how to be compatible and reach alignment on expectations. This is usually doable. It is possible for one to inherit a situation in which alignment is not possible among key stakeholders. In such a case I would argue that it is better to make this determination quickly upfront, as opposed to waiting until a tipping point or event occurs that causes a crisis. Sometime the best that can be done is to escalate the issue up through the management hierarchy— even to the board level, if necessary. And if resolution isn't possible, it may be better to cut your losses and move to a new opportunity as Don Smith, mentioned earlier, did.

A few final parting thoughts: 1) involve your management team, 2) know your stakeholders and proactively manage these relationships, and 3) include this activity in your normal planning algorithm. If you don't manage stakeholders then stakeholder perception will surely manage you. As John Kenneth Galbraith said, "In any great organization it is far, far safer to be wrong with the majority than to be right alone." Investing appropriately in stakeholder management will allow you to take the right path with supportive stakeholders who are endorsing and pulling for your continued success.

Chapter Five Note

1.   Sources: Wikipedia; BusinessDictionary.com.

 **Chapter Six**

Designing a Scalable, Stable, Productive Organization

Organization charts and fancy titles count for next to nothing.
—Colin Powell

It's likely that organization design, or more accurately, organization *re*design, is the most frequently performed planning activity. There are a number of reasons for this but unfortunately most of the reasons companies have for initiating an organization redesign effort are the wrong reasons. For example, companies will instigate a redesign to address such issues as sagging company performance, cost reduction, and global expansion, or to shake up the status quo or improve employee collaboration and alignment. Any one of these conditions could justify an organization redesign effort. But to call organizational design "the foundation of a successful company" is a bunch of baloney. Let me restate my point more explicitly: just about any organization design can work *if*—and that's a big "if"—its leaders and employees are willing to support and work within the overall design. So while effective organization design can contribute to an organization's success, it is not unto itself a direct point of control for the conditions named above.

It's clear that organization design can help facilitate or inhibit the achievement of a strategy. This doesn't mean that if the organization design is sub-optimal the company will fail. It just means that it might take more energy (team and employee sophistication) on everyone's part to work within such a design. And when I speak of organization design, I'm not only speaking of rearranging groups, divisions, units, and reporting structures, I'm also referring to the soft tissue that is the true machinery with which any organization operates: policies, procedures, processes, workflows, interdependencies, communication methods, the decision making processes, and associated authority. Beyond organization charts there is a lot of stuff that also needs to be addressed and re-worked and/or realigned as structures are changed. Herein lies a huge issue: many executives become enthralled with re-

> *"...employees represent a form of organizational currency."*

designing organizations to solve a myriad of problems with enough energy and will to address only the organization charts. Interest drops after that—leaving the managers and employees to figure out ad hoc how to put the balance of the organization back together again. What a mess. This is like trying to fix a flat tire on a car while driving in commute traffic. Why do these superficial, back-of-the-napkin organization design efforts keep occurring (like viruses in many companies)? It's because employees represent a form of organizational currency. Beyond title and pay, the way a leader and his peers measure power and authority is by the number of employees he has in his organization. So, shifting boxes on an organization chart with each box containing "x" number of employees is like playing Monopoly. If you win, you've got a lot of properties (business units) filled with cash (employees). This is also a clear example of how organizational leaders gravitate to running the company from a Dimension Three perspective (Functional)—the powerful fiefdom approach.

Our passion for organizational redesign has a high cost, especially if we engage in it at a critical juncture in the organization's life cycle for the wrong reasons. Short of bankruptcy, takeover, or invasion by space aliens, organization redesign is the most disruptive initiative that leaders can introduce. And, in this vein, it becomes important to understand when to do it and how to do it so that the undertaking and its ensuing organizational impact have the best possible outcome.

Before I move on from this point let me restate several things: 1) organization design is generally a loss leader, meaning it is done for the wrong reasons, 2) redesign efforts tend to be superficial in nature and focus only on structure; as such, the initiative doesn't effectively manage all of the factors and variables necessary to achieve an optimal result, and 3) today's organizations are inherently complex. As Saul Wurman, the futurist, said, "It's not about simplification, it's about clarification." We need to identify and manage all of the variables in a design effort with the goal of setting up an organization structure and associated processes that provide a solid foundation for achievement of the organization's strategy, while minimizing turbulence and other unwanted disturbance in the workforce.

What is the purpose of organization design?

Organizations need flexible structures that can accommodate the dynamic demands of today's business environments. Change is a constant and should be a primary design element incorporated into any company architecture. Organizations need the ability to shift the composition of the workforce (capabilities) and critical mass (numbers of employees) quickly to respond to business challenges. Fixed structures create barriers and bureaucracies and block organizational agility. I'd like to sound prophetic here but this isn't a new observation.

In the early 1980s, IBM popularized a simple matrix organization in which talent resided in functional units (see vertical columns in Figure 6.1 below), but a good portion of work was performed by temporary cross-functional teams driven by project leads (alpha, beta, omega). These teams were created to address and respond to a business need and then disbanded when the work was finished. Employees in the temporary organization never left their functional unit, thus maintaining a degree of purity relative to functional expertise and also being available again for allocation when the next project challenge arose.

Project Lead	Function #1	Function #2	Function #3	Function #4	Function #5
	Sales	Prod Mrktg	Engineering	Manufacturing	Research
Alpha	1*	2	4	2	1
Beta	3	1	3	2	1
Omega	5	1	2	5	1
* number of employees allocated					

Figure 6.1: Deployment Matrix

In this model, it was also possible for a single employee, say a member of the sales function, to be assigned concurrently to two or maybe even three project teams. Most organizations shy away from any such model. Why? Leaders must share power and employees—which, as I noted above, are the currency of a modern-day organization. It also requires advanced citizenship to live and work inside an organizational construct such as this. It needs sophisticated performance management, communication, and compensation processes. Leaders and managers need to have advanced negotiation and influence skills. Employees must be comfortable with multiple supervisors and ready for a bit more ambiguity injected into the day-to-day routine. I've heard this described as "serving many masters" or "having multiple marriages." No wonder it hasn't caught on in a big way. We're still tangled up in who has the most ceiling tiles (i.e., the biggest office), the most direct reports, and the most impressive title.

With the pervasive use of organization redesign as the one-size-fits-all solution, it's too bad that it actually has little to do with improving an organization's performance. In fact, my

> *"In a changing or unstable environment, productivity can drop below 43%."*

last client, a hi-tech software firm in Silicon Valley, had reorganized its software engineering group seven times in four years. The last reorganization was still in motion when I left. It had been in process for over five months. If this isn't torturing employees and disrupting work focus, I'm not sure what is. The apparent catalysts for all those reorganizations were leadership changes, product portfolio shifts, and attempts to address poor overall divisional quality and performance issues.

Productivity is impacted by organizational change

Consider this: work force productivity sits at about 74% in a stable environment[1]. In a changing or unstable environment, productivity can drop below 43%. Let those numbers simmer in your head for a minute. Now add other factors into the equation. For instance, following the announcement for organizational change, it takes weeks to months for employees to work through, internalize, and adapt to the changes. This assumes that the organization design work is done efficiently so that teams can immediately start to assimilate new requirements, and reform and stabilize after the change event. But many reorganizations are not efficient. These events tend to be what I term "blunt instruments of change," beginning with countless leadership meetings, negotiations, and compromises. By the time agreement is reached on the new organization design, the employee rumor mill is already in full swing and has rehashed every possible change scenario and the worst-case-possible outcomes. This, unfortunately, is an innate human characteristic: to contemplate worst-case scenarios and gossip about them with associates. Even if the new organization design provides a better working structure, many employees are completely stressed-out, frustrated, frantic, and caught up contemplating the ultimate question, "How does this impact me?" So, an effective reorganization design effort had better answer that "How does this impact me?" question upfront and quickly. A perfect example of this occurred while I was completing this manuscript: HP's new CEO, Leo Apotheker, had just announced that the company strategy was shifting to focus on the more profitable commercial tech business. In doing so, he shared that HP's flagship personal computer division may be sold or spun out into a separate company. About 100,000 of HP's global workforce of 300,000 employees are engaged in building and selling PCs. HP's stock took a 20% hit, wiping out $12 billion of the company's value. Leo noted to analysts that the PC division may not be sold—in making his announcement, he had just wanted to share his early thinking upfront—and that it would likely take up to a year to make the correct decision. Will this

> "...many reorganizations are not efficient."

announcement impact employee productivity, accountability, and retention? Has it already? Will customers want to make large purchases of HP PCs that might have an uncertain product future? Will top talent come to the PC division? Will the best-performing employees stay? Postscript: Leo was fired by the board of directors just a few days after making his announcement due to shareholder pressure.

The productivity/people impact of organizational redesign is so extreme that I would caution any leader, "Don't engage in this activity unless absolutely necessary. If you do, make sure you have a clear strategy that necessitates this dramatic move and that there is a well-articulated process (with a communication plan on steroids) to follow that will limit the amount of time it takes, from start to finish."

General observations on organization design

▷ Organization design is not a panacea. Make no mistake, even if performed well, it will be highly disruptive to the organization. Bigger productivity gains are made through improved teaming schemes, didactic communication, and refinement of systems and processes to support such an environment. Make sure the organizational design effort targets teaming, communication, alignment of adjacent and necessary work groups, and the core processes, policies, programs, and decision making protocol that go with the structure.

▷ Author Laura Ingalls Wilder once said, "The trouble with organizing a thing is that pretty soon folks get to paying more attention to the organization than to what [it is that] they're organized for." Don't allow organization design efforts to become a defocusing element wherein leader and manager accountability is lost. A single redesign effort can consume thousands of person hours, reduce or stop project progress for months, escalate unwanted attrition, and send the wrong message to customers, stakeholders, competitors, and potential employees. Employee accountability tends to disappear during an extensive redesign effort—another reason that this activity has such a high impact on productivity.

▷ Organization redesign gives leaders a false sense of accomplishment. They observe that furious activity was generated. A momentary focus was created. Another project was checked off as completed on a metrics chart. But, what was really achieved in the overall scheme of things? So, make sure that there is a clear understanding of the cause and effect of such an effort. If you must conduct an organization design effort, be certain that it is being performed for the right reasons at the right time with the right process.

What are the wrong reasons and least optimal timing to reorganize?

Before embarking on an organization design, make sure you're not doing it for any of the following wrong reasons and that your timing is spot on.

1. If the strategy is unclear or unstable, don't reorganize. Doing so is building a house on a foundation of sand. Invest time first clarifying the strategic context. Only then are leaders ready to ask, "What are the strategic implications about how we organize the company?" and "What design best enables the achievement of the strategy?" Many times merely tweaking the current organization structure will do fine. It's not glamorous, melodramatic, or sexy, but it may be the best-case scenario for the company and the path that the leader should follow.

2. Don't reorganize until your leadership team is truly a team. If you have an influx of new leaders from inside or external to the organization, then the first order of business is team building. That way, the input, participation, and general thinking that goes into an organization design effort will be of higher quality and more likely that the output (i.e., new organization model) will be endorsed by the team.

3. Don't use reorganization as a tool to cut costs and/or address legacy employee performance issues. This is like hunting with a shotgun when a high-powered rifle (with pinpoint accuracy) is needed. In those instances when organization redesign must be used to address these topics, don't change the organization chart per se. Focus on the policies, procedures, programs, and performance management elements. This minimizes overall company disruption. Also, if poor performance is the primary motivation to initiate a redesign effort, this invariably shifts the focus to designing around available people as opposed to designing around the overall strategic needs of an organization. Mixing these activities tends to eliminate objectivity in the organization design process and guarantees that the next organization redesign isn't too far off in the future.

4. Never redesign an organization with an interim leader or with key leaders missing from the equation. Leaders generally have a predisposition for the type of organizational structure that they feel most comfortable working within. If the design work is done without pivotal input from the ultimate owners and drivers of the organization, you can bet that another reorganization will be in motion soon.

5. Avoid using reorganization as a cost-effectiveness and/or performance-improvement tool when the root cause of the problem is unclear. It's possible that the best thing the company

has working for it is its organization design. If the organization design isn't the root cause, don't change it. As noted earlier, it seems that leadership is always fiddling with organization designs as a way to amp up productivity or to cut costs. Organization charts rarely have a lot to do with these two topics—it's all of the behind-the-scenes infrastructure (processes, policies, procedures, programs) and how people work together that is ultimately the culprit.

I'm not against organization design activity per se. I have paid my bills and fed my family for many years designing and redesigning organizations. I'm against using organization design for the wrong reasons, since the employee impact is always significant. Effective organization design is my passion and a topic that I've spent a major portion of my work life trying to master. Like many of my peers, I have also spent a great deal of time working on organization redesign when I suspected upfront that there was a high likelihood that the effort wasn't addressing the root cause—thus all of the effort could end up for naught. An ethical external consultant will walk away from these projects. On the other hand, internal consultants, employed by the company, many times need to just suck it up and perform the work hoping that down the road other opportunities to get it right will surface.

How to design the organization for stability and productivity

This section is dedicated entirely to the "how-to" for creating an effective organization design. In presenting this material, I'm working on the assumption that it makes sense to redesign the organization—based on the input that I provided above. Effective organization design addresses many aspects: company structure, organization charts, reporting, lines of authority, interdependencies, workflows, related programs, processes, accountabilities, communication channels, and decision making. This is the internal machinery of organizations. The degree to which this machinery is aligned and working in support of the company's strategy is a key determinant of success. When the machinery of the organization is jumbled and working against itself, it turns the work environment into a place of guerilla warfare, i.e., employees need to spend significant amounts of time and energy working around the system to get things done. Most of us have had this experience in our adult working life and we scratch our heads and say, "Wow, are the leaders nuts? Do they know how complicated it is to work here? It seems like I spend most of my time figuring out how to get things done rather than accomplishing the job that I was hired to do." Does this sound at all familiar?

I've focused this section on effective organizational design, but I've stopped short of addressing workflows, processes, and communication channels. I think these are straightforward once the macro design effort is complete. This method is a scalable process, i.e., it can be used to design a company, a division of that company, or even a grouping of business units within a large division. In all of these scenarios, the same principles apply.

Rules of Design

The starting point is agreement about methodology. The "rules of design" noted below should be fixed parameters when initiating organization redesign:

▷ *Create organizational designs first; save people selection for later*

Who goes in what box on the prototype organization charts is not an appropriate discussion until organizational modeling is complete. It is common practice to design organizations around available people. This tactic undermines effective design. Once multiple designs have been created and capabilities identified for key positions in the new model (independent of people selection), then a deliberate and calculated matching of available candidates can be performed in an objective manner. If the exact match for a respective position doesn't exist in the organization, then a decision can be made to offer the position to the best internal candidate (with the condition of a development plan and associated time frame for achievement) or to fill the position with an external candidate who more closely matches the required skill set.

▷ *A clear business strategy is an essential starting point*

Redesigning the organization structure can be a sub-optimized endeavor if it feeds from a poorly articulated strategy. If the organization design process raises concerns about the clarity and quality of the business strategy, stop and reinvest in strategic planning. As noted earlier, starting to work on a company's organizational structure while its strategy is unclear or in flux will certainly lead to premature redesign efforts sure to cause disruption in the work environment.

▷ *Form a balanced design team*

Planning the composition of a design team is critical. Look for a balanced group of participants with knowledge of the industry, knowledge of the company, a willingness to participate, and the ability to "think outside the box." The highest-level sponsor endorsing the work should always be included. The executive team—those reporting to the CEO or company leader—is not necessarily the best organization design planning team. Members from that group may be too invested in a particular outcome to be objective. However, all members of the executive team should always provide input and feedback.

▷ *Stay with the process*

The process outlined on the pages that follow has 10 steps. A number of variables will affect how long the process will take to complete: gathering data, reviewing work with stakeholders, getting the planning team assembled for several different meetings, etc. The tendency in design work is to over-compress or short-circuit the steps. Remember, a subordinated process will yield subordinated results. Effective organization design doesn't have to take a lot of chronological or cumulative time. Many planning efforts bog down when the road map is not clear or is not followed from start to finish. As noted, I have outlined a 10-step road map here that has proven itself in over 150 design efforts. The road map helps to keep the effort focused, timely, and results-oriented. Note: Unless an organization design expert is on the team, don't spend time "designing or redesigning the design process itself." This is not a high-value activity and presents the possibility that the process followed may not yield the desired result.

▷ *Do not expect the new organization designs to be a panacea*

As discussed earlier, organization redesign tends to be motivated by the need to cut costs, improve communications, speed time to market, get closer to the customer, assimilate acquired companies, and justify the elimination of certain jobs and positions. While a new design can help facilitate all of these things, it does not come without cost. The transition from the old business architecture to the new business architecture can be expensive and might require fundamental shifts in the approach to and delivery of products and services to customers. A new organizational design can necessitate huge restructuring charge-offs (resulting in reduced quarterly earnings and stock price) and may temporarily disrupt service to the customer base or force standardization of products and services that restrict specialized treatment of certain customer segments, i.e., a decentralized product division company can usually provide all things to all customers (a philosophical orientation to doing business) while a front/back-organized company will find it more difficult to behave the same way because its structure tends to rely on a higher degree of product standardization. Be open to keeping the current organization design and simply fine-tuning a few aspects of it to achieve the desired result. If the analysis is performed objectively, this could be a possible outcome. Change for the sake of change doesn't necessarily solve existing problems and may create new ones.

▷ *Maintain line-of-sight structures whenever possible*

We are in the information age with many new forms of gadgets that supposedly promote communication: video conferencing, texting, voicemail, email, facebook, twitter—with more surely to come. However, nothing has changed when it comes to how people work most effectively together. We are social creatures who require "human interaction." New technologies haven't replaced or altered the need for human beings to interact formally and informally to work effectively together. This is one area where organization design can make a huge contribution. Whenever possible, choose design elements that maintain employee line-of-sight, i.e., keep employees who are performing the same work or performing one element of the same task together in the same organization or design a matrix organization that creates the right interconnections/relationships. Don't think that goodwill and teamwork can make up for organization designs that isolate and separate natural work groups. Also, make sure to organizationally cluster employee units that have a high degree of interdependency on achieving objectives. Carving up logical groupings of employees and scattering them across geographies and lines of authority promote the guerilla warfare condition discussed earlier. This builds inefficiency into the organization on the front end.

The organization design process

Below is a 10-step organization design process (Figure 6.2) that follows a critical path, i.e., complete step one before proceeding to step two. This represents approximately a 10-hour time commitment from design team members.

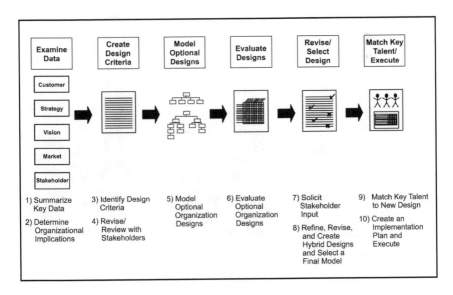

Figure 6.2: 10-Step Organization Design Process

1. Collate Data Point and Master Plan information

When an architect considers building a house, the first place to begin is with a solid foundation. It is important to identify what you know and what you potentially may need to know in order to create the right design for your organization. An easy first step is to draw on the company's strategic planning work. Relevant strategic documents, including the Data Points, should be considered when engaging in design work. If this information is not available, then assemble what is available. Then determine if it makes sense to proceed. If yes, use the intellect of the planning team to fill in any gaps, i.e., if Data Points are missing, then brainstorm as a group to surface the pertinent information for each area. Make sure that all planning members have the same packet of information for review. Refer to Chapter Two for suggested plan documents. If this information isn't available from a previous strategic planning activity, then it will need to be created here for this purpose and validated with relevant stakeholders.

2. Determine the organizational implications for each Data Point, Mission and Master Plan

Each Data Point contains clues about how the organization must behave in order to be effective. Examine each Data Point and try to decipher the organizational characteristics it may require, e.g., a customer Data Point might contain information that suggests that it's critically important that the company is co-located with key customers; this should be highlighted and included as a characteristic that is important to the organization design effort.

3. Identify organization design criteria

Organization design criteria guide the design effort and help evaluate whether the end product, a new organization design, will support the strategy—the ultimate purpose of organization design. According to

Jay Galbraith, "...design criteria are concrete statements on how the organization will behave." Examples of design criteria are: 1) we will deliver product "x" no later than 24 hours after the customer has ordered it, 2) we need a sales office in every Asia-based country where we do business, or 3) we want to reduce layers of management that stand between an employee and the CEO to minimize hierarchy.

Here are additional examples of design criteria that can help stimulate thinking for the design team:

▷ Enable clearly defined roles and responsibilities

▷ Organization structure must support the drive for cost reduction and continuous improvement

▷ Increase capability of focusing efforts into emerging market opportunities

▷ Co-locate/increase presence in key markets

▷ Be customer-driven (which allows access to key customers for engineering, product marketing, and R&D)

Design teams will settle on five to eight design criteria that are the most critical characteristics that the ultimate design would support.

4.   Review and revise design criteria based on stakeholder input

Once design criteria have been identified, these need to be reviewed with stakeholders for input and buy-in. Stakeholders will make additions and deletions and provide general comments that will reveal closely held predispositions. If stakeholders have not been previously identified in an overarching planning process, it will be necessary to stop here and do so. Do not skip this step. It is undesirable to be in a position where you need to sell a new organization design to a key stakeholder (someone who needs to approve or buy in to the new design) at the end of the process. Including stakeholders early on in the design activity serves as a way to build support and ultimately gain approval, plus it helps develop an understanding of stakeholder wants and needs so that these can be addressed during the design activity. This approach accomplishes several key goals: 1) stakeholders are involved in the process, which ultimately helps them own and accept the final result, 2) stakeholders may be holding critical information; asking for input can unveil this information, and 3) stakeholders will be tuned in and able to provide valuable in-context comments and input later on (during step #7) if they are engaged on the front end.

5. Model optional organization designs

Based on design criteria, draw several organizational models starting first with a graphic structure and next (using bullet points) a description of the unique aspects of how this organization operates. Make sure to include the existing organizational model as one of the designs. This will be used as a base line for comparison and evaluation purposes. (See Figure 6.3 as an example of formatting)

Modeling helps map and clearly define potential organizational architectures. It is a fleshing-out process. Usually one or more leaders has a specific organizational model in mind. That's great. Record the model. If leaders are unclear about where to begin, start by 1) designing the most centralized model that can be imagined that could possibly work, 2) then designing the most decentralized model that could work, and 3) trying alternative designs such as a matrix organization or a process organization. It is important to keep the modeling activity going until four or five different models are created. This promotes out-of-the-box thinking. All models must include the visible structure and then a list of bullet points on the bottom that denotes the key characteristics of this particular design. This helps the design team and others not engaged in the design process understand the thinking and mechanics of the design.

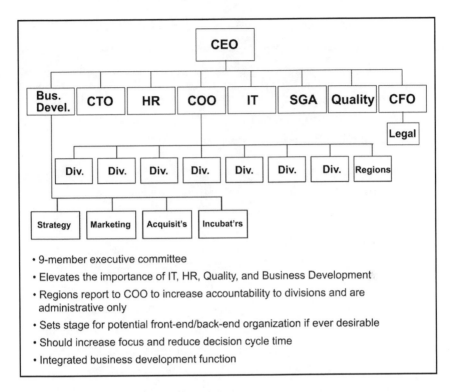

Figure 6.3: Functional Organization

The model above illustrates a functional organization wherein employees and activities are grouped according to their function and functional units and structured under the general manager of a business.

Some additional general organization models are described below. A "good" organization design doesn't necessarily need to fall clearly into a well-known organizational classification (as defined below). What is important is that the organization design will optimally serve the company's strategy. These definitions help us with the semantics of design work and provide a general reference to categories of organizational layouts. There are an infinite number of design variations. No two organizations are alike in regard to their strategy and organizational needs, and thus their organizational structure. Here are several broad organizational archetypes:

▷ *Product Organization*: an organization arranged according to product units or lines of business that report to the general manager of the business.

▷ *Worldwide Regional Organization*: an organization that divides the globe into regional units, each of which has control over all business activities in its geographic area.

▷ *Mixed/Hybrid Organization*: a structure that includes two or more organization formats within the same business unit; for example, a country, two lines of business, and/or several functions all reporting to the general manager.

▷ *Matrix Organization*: an organization that attempts to balance and integrate the roles and responsibilities of product, geographic, and functional units in the administrative structure of business. To succeed, the organization depends upon the implementation of a unique set of behaviors of corporate or business unit culture. Here, teamwork is paramount—systems that promote and reward teamwork are a critical precondition.

▷ *Process Organization*: a flat performance-based organization comprising horizontal core business processes carried out by multifunctional teams often led by a process owner. In this decentralized format, the hierarchy of the business unit plays more of a supportive than a control role.

▷ *Lateral Organization*: an organization that consists of horizontal cross-functional processes that cross hierarchical lines, i.e., a process organization with a strong hierarchical overlay. The lateral processes can be informal, voluntary, and spontaneous, or they can be formal and explicit.

▷ *Front-End/Back-End Organization*: an organization in which some functions are aggregated on the front end of the business to serve customers, and other functions are clustered on the back end to develop and create products. A key organizational task is finding ways to integrate the activities of both ends.

▷ *Functional Organization*: an organization where employee units and lines of authority and activities are grouped according to traditional functional areas, such as, Manufacturing, Product Development, and Sales & Marketing. It's very typical for a CEO to have all functional heads reporting to her (those areas named above), including support functions such as Finance, Human Resources, Information Technologies, etc.

Figure 6.4 is an example of a front-end/back-end organization in which regional responsibility is shared with division sales managers (i.e., the wearing of two hats).

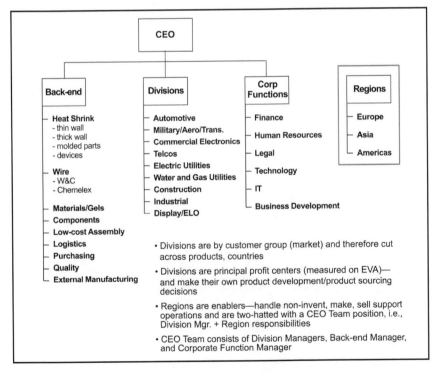

Figure 6.4: Front-end/Back-end Organization

Figure 6.5 is what I term a modified functional organization. This removes the CEO from the heart of the manufacturing business and support functions (which frees up a lot of time) by shifting responsibility to a chief operating officer, but insulates the CEO from some of the dynamics of the business. This is neither good nor bad, but it could be risky especially if the manufacturing side of the business is not stable.

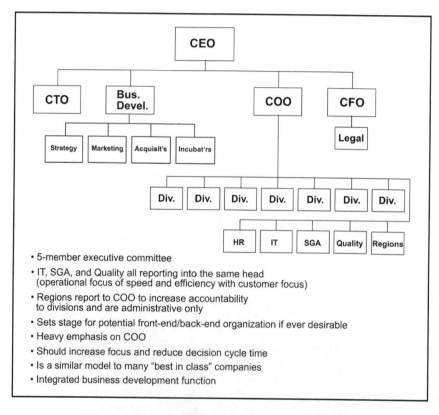

Figure 6.5: Modified Functional Organization

If the design team has difficulty coming up with a variety of ways to structure the company, provide a thinking catalyst by asking them to translate their current organization into one of the general organizational models previously described, i.e., try designing a front-back or matrix organization. As noted earlier, another way to stimulate the group's design creativity is ask members of the group to design the most centralized organization that they can imagine and then contrast that work with the most decentralized organization possible. Creating a variety of diverse designs is important. Contrasting these diverse designs against one another during the evaluation phase will add richness to the discussion and possibly unveil viable design options not under consideration previously.

6. Evaluate optional organizations

Once a variety of prototype organizations has been modeled, evaluate these prototypes against the design criteria (Figure 6.6 below). This effort will likely lead to model derivations—moving the design thought process to breakthrough and hybrid models. It is important to include some designs that may appear too extreme or countercultural in this step. Make sure that the design effort has produced some provocative models. It is very common to discover an organization model that hadn't been envisioned prior to this activity.

In Figure 6.6, seven design criteria were used to evaluate seven organizational models described by a design team. Figures 6.3, 6.4, & 6.5 earlier in this chapter represent design A, design C and design D, respectively. The potential organizational types included two functional models, two front-back models, a product model, a process model, and a mixed or hybrid model.

A number of interesting revelations surfaced during the evaluation process shown in Figure 6.6: 1) the organization design that scored the highest was a front-back model; this ultimately proved unsalable to stakeholders because it was such a radical departure from the current organization, 2) role definition and lines of authority with any organizational type would be critical; at this point, modeling activity didn't give a good feel about what would be required to implement one of the new designs, and 3) the team was more objective with evaluation than it thought was possible; team members attributed this to not being tainted by the "people aspect" when considering the best alternative organizational designs.

The highest-scoring organizational type is not necessarily the "best" or most appropriate organization for today. Many factors will play into the final selection. What the design process helps accomplish is that it systematically captures the best thinking of the design team and supports any design decision with as much relevant, pertinent data as possible.

Organization Design Criteria	1-Design A	2-Design B	3-Design C	4-Design D	5-Design E	6-Design F	7-Design G	Weighting
1) Customer-driven – "Doing what the customer wants"	5	2	4	3	3	4	5	
2) Clearly defined roles and responsibilities that can flex to the changing needs of the company	4	3	5	1	4	2	3	2x
3) Enhances decision making process: speed and efficiency	3	3	4	2	4	2	3	
4) Capable of focusing effort into emerging market opportunities	4	3	4	2	4	1	3	2x
5) Organization structure must support the drive for cost reduction and continuous improvement	3	3	4	3	3	3	1	
6) Recognize, reward, and nurture innovation and prudent risk-taking	3	2	4	4	3	3	2	
7) Organization must have built-in mechanisms to constantly redefine itself	3	3	3	3	3	3	3	
Totals	**33**	**25**	**37**	**21**	**32**	**21**	**26**	

5 = high (Organization Design promotes/supports this design criterion)
3 = neutral (Organization Design could promote or inhibit this design criterion)
1 = low (Organization Design inhibits/undermines this design criterion)

Figure 6.6: Evaluation Matrix

Note: Evaluate the organization models together with the design team, face to face. Evaluate each organization design, one at a time, using a scale of 1 to 5. Also note that the far right "weighting" column in the matrix is used to skew the value of design criteria, i.e., two or three criteria identified may be more important or more critical for the organization than the others. Give these a two- or three-"x" rating (2x or 3x). Score the matrix horizontally first to incorporate the exponential weighting, then add it vertically.

7. Solicit stakeholder input

With data in hand, stakeholders are asked for their thoughts, impressions, concerns, etc., about the conclusions the design effort has produced. This can uncover new insights and help refine the design work. It also locks the stakeholders into the ultimate solution. This is highly desirable since introducing new infrastructure usually causes distress and creates issues that ultimately impact stakeholders. Stakeholder buy-in helps keep the environment stable (on task) while any tough choices and decisions are being implemented.

8. Refine/revise/develop hybrid organization model; select alpha organization

Once stakeholder input has been received, a final organization model is selected and refined. If this requires approval or a joint decision from outside the design team, arrange for a briefing session.

At the completion of this step it's time to match key talent to the new organization. Rather than designate which people belong in which boxes on an ad hoc basis (which might seem like the most straightforward way to do it), an intermediate step is recommended: define the key characteristics for each position identified in the new organization design and then select people who best match those characteristics.

9. Select and match key talent to the alpha organization

Up to this point in the design process, names of people that go in boxes are not considered in any way. The focus has been on designing the best organizational model to deliver against the company's strategic plan. Sometimes leaders will approach a selection process of this nature with disdain, e.g., "I don't need a committee to help me fill in an organization chart." Yet, unless the organization is extremely small (less than 200 employees), it can be difficult to know if the right person with the right characteristics is actually being matched to the job. Some degree of exploration and discussion anchored into performance expectations for a key position helps vet the "right people for the right job" selection process. Unless leaders are willing to engage in this way, good design work can be undermined. The process detailed here is quick and efficient and will help leverage a company's selection and placement program (or succession plan).

There are five separate potential activities to this step: 1) identify the key objectives of the job, 2) given those objectives, identify the key characteristics (capabilities) an individual must possess to be successful in this role, 3) ask appropriate stakeholders for input/refinement, 4) identify a candidate slate—these are potential candidates who have been pre-qualified by both Human Resources and the appropriate technical, functional, or business unit manager, and 5) evaluate the candidates against the key characteristics.

"Sometimes leaders will approach a selection process of this nature with disdain..."

Figures 6.7 and 6.8 (below) show the final output of step #9: select and match key talent with the alpha organization. The individual with the highest numerical score doesn't automatically get the job. Hopefully, the hiring manager participated in the process and will have learned a great deal about the expected performance of the individual placed in the position and will make a relatively objective decision in the best interests of the organization.

A common question is, "What if we identify desirable characteristics for key positions and then find that we don't have adequate

Marketing/Sales Executive Candidate Evaluation

Key objectives of job:

- Take a lead in enhancing TQM programs in sales and marketing
- Represent the sales and marketing people of Raychem
- Benchmark company against leading sales and marketing companies
- Direct, with Human Resources, sales training programs throughout the world
- Oversight of Americas, Euro, and Asia sales and marketing committees
- Drive to eliminate roadblocks to cross-division selling
- Set up and monitor costs related to selling and marketing of our products
- Develop systems to enhance market research skills throughout the company
- Develop systems to enhance sales forecasting skills throughout the company

Identification of potential candidates (or "Candidate Slate"):

- Joe Taft
- Kathy Bernstein
- Lori Sims
- Michael Emerson
- Sue Blake

Candidate evaluation against key leadership characteristics:

Key Characteristics	Taft	Bernstein	Sims	Emerson	Blake			Weighting
1) Sales/Marketing "union card" at company	5	5	3	4	4			(2x)
2) International experience	3	4	4	3	3			
3) Strong process skills	3	3	5	5	4			
4) Integrating personality: manage by influence/ broad perspective	4	3	2	4	3			(2x)
5) Passion for training and updating sales and marketing skills	3	3	3	3	3			
6) Candidate for further development	4	1	2	4	5			
(5 = high, 0 = low) M/S Totals	31	27	24	31	29			

Figure 6.7: Marketing Sales/Executive Candidate Evaluation

skills in-house to fill these roles?" Depending on the nature of the position, there are several ways to address this: 1) Thoroughly search the organization for qualified candidates even if it is thought that they don't exist—larger organizations tend to have a hierarchical view of their own people, i.e., people at lower levels in the organization have lower-level skills, knowledge, motives, and general capability; this is a false assumption and worth challenging since many CEOs of Fortune 500 companies started in the mailroom. 2) Sub-optimize the position by putting someone in the role who doesn't have the requisite qualifications, i.e., have a technical manager with no direct marketing education or experience assume the newly created job of "marketing manager." Do so conditionally—give the employee goals, objectives, and a development period. If the development objectives aren't reached in the required time frame, then remove him from

> *"...sub-optimize the position by placing a high-potential individual in it..."*

the job; that way, a long, drawn-out performance management process isn't required. 3) Sub-optimize the position by placing a high-potential individual in it who only partially meets the job requirements (very typical corporate movement pattern for high potentials)—this is done with the understanding that certain skill and knowledge deficiencies must be addressed immediately to maintain the role. 4) Fill the position from outside the company, which may cause the displacement of internal people. The decision point here should be straightforward if a thorough analysis has been done to identify the key characteristics or needs of the job. Ask these questions, "Can our company afford less than a 100% impact player in this job today?" "In six months?" "Maybe never?" "Would filling this position with an external candidate have a positive or negative effect on the existing team?" How these questions

Manufacturing Staff Executive Candidate Evaluation

Key objectives of job:

- Take the lead in enhancing TQM programs in manufacturing
- Represent the manufacturing people of company
- Benchmark Company against leading manufacturing companies
- Oversight of Americas and Europe Marcoms
- Direct, with Human Resources, manufacturing training programs throughout the world
- Represent manufacturing in IT issues

Identification of potential candidates:

- Jim Chen
- Bill McCulsky
- Martha Swanson
- Betty Huvana
- Dave Ries
- Samantha Westrum
  (candidacy identified but not evaluated)

Candidate evaluation against key leadership characteristics:

Key Characteristics	Chen	McCulsky	Swanson	Huvana	Ries			Weighting
1) Manufacturing "union card"	5	3	4	4	2			
2) International experience	4	5	5	5	4			
3) Integrating personality: manage by influence/ broad perspective	4	3	4	3	3			(2x)
4) Ability to identify and transfer "best in class" manufacturing technologies	5	4	5	4	4			
5) Passion for training and updating manufacturing skills	5	5	4	5	5			
6) Candidate for further development	4	2	4	4	3			
7) Stature in organization	5	2	4	5	3			
(5 = high, 0 = low) M/S Totals	36	27	34	33	27			

Figure 6.8: Manufacturing Staff Executive Candidate Evaluation

are answered determines the different paths that can be taken to get there.

Identification of the key characteristics of any given position is similar to identifying organization design criteria. It is probably appropriate and necessary to use outside input (such as stakeholders who have unique insight into a given position) to help shape these position descriptions—especially for high-visibility, high-impact roles.

Usually the selection and approval of key executives have CEO and board of directors involvement. It is important that the right mix of people is involved in the evaluation process. It is also important that the hiring manager have the final say as to who gets the job. Many times a gut feeling or "chemistry" plays a critical role in the selection process. This is why the scoring on the matrix is not an absolute. The highest-scoring candidate may not be the best person for the job. The purpose here is to drive the selection process by the needs of the organization—to systematically surface those needs—and minimize favoritism, politics, and other organizational traits that so often promote mediocrity in the selection and placement process.

10. Develop an implementation/transition plan

As a final planning step, the design team should consider how to best mete out the plan into the organization. What will be the protocol? What are the significant milestones? What are the indicators of success? How can a positive transition be facilitated, knowing that many organizational renewal efforts fail during implementation?

Step #10 is crucial and cannot be adequately addressed in the scope of this document. Best case, this organization design work has been done within the context of an overall transition planning process. If so, implementation planning is already part of the scheme. If not, I recommend reading pages 129–145 of *The Transition Equation: A Proven Strategy for Organizational Change* (J. Allan McCarthy,

Lexington Books, an imprint of Free Press–Simon and Schuster, 1995) or locate an excerpt at www.mccarthyandaffiliates.com.

Here are some additional thoughts if this organization design work is to be performed independent of an overarching transition planning process.

▷ Any time a planning team forms, the organization will know about it. So tell employees what you are going to do and why you are going to do it prior to beginning. Let the employee population know what to expect, when the next communication will be received, and then stick with the schedule. It seems that leaders involved in organization design work tend to forget that the balance of the organization is waiting and watching and even stewing over possible outcomes. Therefore, timely communication with specific intent and outcomes is important. This shouldn't be viewed as an elective activity; for the welfare of all concerned, commit to it and do it.

▷ Design work, especially when performed top-down, will "freak out" even the most senior employees. People will immediately become concerned about job security. The anxiety that accompanies any activity of this nature can be minimized (very important in terms of productivity) if the objective(s), milestones, and potential outcomes are disclosed upfront. People settle down when they know what to expect. Even when many employees, from senior to junior ranks, stand to be ousted or redeployed, anxiety can be curbed by having straightforward mechanisms in place to handle the unknowns, i.e., the biggest anxiety producer is "What happens if I lose my job?" The answer: if you are displaced, here is information on: 1) when you will know, 2) how much time you will have to find another job, 3) your parting benefits, and 4) how the company will help you with your transition.

> ▷ Research shows that companies that are extremely proactive in the management of reorganization and displacement activities maintain high morale (even in the worst circumstances) and suffer less subsequent loss of key talent. In other words, it is cost-effective to expend "great effort" in the care and treatment of people during transition.

The heavy lifting of organization design

If the design team stayed with the process described above there's a chance that a relatively stable organization design has emerged. That's the high-level structural fun stuff that leaders like to do but it's far from completing the overall design process. I won't detail all of the aspects here but will spend a few moments to discuss those items that need attention next. These are:

1. Communicating and socializing the results, first with those most positively and negatively impacted by the new design, second with the larger organization, and finally with stakeholders who likely need or want to know about changes. This could include customers, analysts, and partners.

2. Resetting the organization has a ripple effect and can substantially impact workflows and organizational processes, team composition (common objectives and interdependencies), lines of communication, decision making processes, and project and product owners and their lines of authority and reporting structures, etc. This is a big "etc." here and it's critically important that a transition team is assembled to manage the immense transition that is triggered by a new organization structure. This represents exponentially more work effort and certainly more people involvement than doing the original structural design work. A warning: do not leave

this to chance, letting the organization work through this informally. In doing so thousands of person hours will be burned off needlessly by employees trying to figure out how to navigate the new landscape—guerilla warfare at its best.

3. Make sure that all leaders and managers who have been installed (promoted or moved) into new jobs are equipped for these jobs. An explicit development plan needs to accompany a promotion or movement of an employee into a critical assignment—one in which she is unproven. Identify performance milestones for the next 12 to 18 months. That way the employee gets the best support possible to ensure success, plus the company will recognize success or failure sooner and can make a change more easily if the person isn't working out.

4. Map and compare old objectives and accountabilities with the new in order to make sure that no balls are dropped during the maze of reorganization activity.

I have found that the following key activities need to immediately follow an organization restructuring: 1) team-build with the new teams with the purpose of identifying common objectives and interdependencies, 2) complete a decision matrix, and 3) launch an internal communications campaign to re-enroll all employees (not just those impacted) on company strategy, the benefits of the organization design effort, and next steps. Make sure to answer these questions that just about every employee has in mind: "How does this impact me?" and "What's in this for me?" Don't underestimate the potential confusion, fear, and anxiety that an employee experiences during a change event—even if the event is well-planned and well-communicated.

The decision matrix effort will also further clarify and promote rapid alignment of workflows, processes, lines of authority, etc., since most activities going on inside an organization have some chain of command involved for sponsorship, accountability, and approval.

How to create a Decision Matrix

I have used several formats for the creation of Decision Matrices. Depending on the complexity of the organization, this can be a challenging task. However, it is amazing how well an activity such as this helps the players sort things out after change. It reduces confusion quickly and forces the new team structures to debate, work through, and reach agreement on how information will flow, who is accountable for what, and how decisions will be made relative to processes and programs.

The traditional models are RACI or CAIRO. RACI is an abbreviation for: R = Responsible to drive and lead the task, A = Approves or in the approval chain for a task, C = Consult with prior to decision, and I = Inform after the decision. The CAIRO acronym is deciphered the same as the RACI model with the exception of the "O," which stands for non sequitur or not relevant for this task. Note: I used the CAIRO model earlier in Chapter Four.

Create a decision matrix by listing the company's core processes, programs, and initiatives in the vertical left-hand margin. Then list leaders, managers, and other stakeholders (on the horizontal axis) who are likely involved in the activities listed in the left-hand margin. Finally, as a planning team, complete the RACI or CAIRO using the appropriate letter that corresponds with the type of activity required from the stakeholder.

I have included an example of an extremely complex stakeholder decision matrix (Figure 6.9) created when a global Fortune 500 software organization developed a global Shared Services model. This activity, of course, had a dramatic impact on how decisions were made, process and

AREA / TOPIC	ROLE [1]								
	Global	BA / LoB		Labs		Corporate HR Services			Other [5]
	HRLT	HR BP	LoB Head	MD	HR	P&G	CoE	HRdirect	Legal, F&A, etc.
Compensation & Benefits									
● Strategy & Policies	A [4]	C	–	–	C	R	R	–	C
● Compensation Framework	C	C	–	–	C	A/R	R	–	C
● Benefits Framework	C	C	–	–	C	A/R	R	–	C
● Local Salary Determination (for MMOs excl. MD) [2]		R	C	A	R		C	–	C
● Local Salary Determination (for MMMs and below) [2]		–	C	A	R	R	C	–	
● Local Salary Determination (VIP) [6]		R	C	A	R	C	C	–	
● Local Bonus Plan Design		C	C	A	R	C	C	–	C
● Local Bonus Plan Execution		–		–	A/R		C	R	
● Local Alignment		C		C	A/R		C	–	C
Global Job Catalogue									
● Framework / Creation	C	C	–	–	C	A/R	R	–	C
● Maintenance		–			–	A	C	R	
● Local Alignment		C		–	R	A/R	A/R	–	C
Job Titles [3]									
● Local Framework		C	–	A	R		R	–	C
● Execution		–		–	A/R		C	–	
Promotions (excl. GEP Moves)									
● Local Framework		C	–	A	R		R	–	C
● Execution		–		–	A/R		C	–	C
Global Mobility									
● Framework / Creation	C	C	–	–	C	A/R	R	–	C
● Local Decision		C	C	A	R	C	C	–	
● Execution		–		–	–	C	A/R	–	
● Local Alignment		C		A	A	C	R	–	C
Employee Terminations									
● BA / LoB initiated termination		R	A	C	R	A/R	R	–	C
● Labs initiated termination		C	C	A	R		C	–	C
Headcount Control		R	A	C	R		R		R

Abbreviations in Chart: A = Accountable; C = Consult; I = Inform; R = Responsible

Abbreviations in Headers: BA = Board Area; CoE = Center of Expertise; F&A = Finance & Administration; GEP = Global Executive Position; HRLT = HR Leadership Team; LoB = Line of Business; MD = Managing Director; MMM = Manager Managing Managers; MMO = Manager Managing Organizations; P&G = Practices & Governance

Footnotes: 1) Escalation Process to be defined; 2) Excludes VIP Process; 3) Not connected to C&B; 4) Joint accountability due to organizational structure; 5) Depending on situation; 6) As long as there is no true Global Executive Compensation Process

Figure 6.9: RACI Decision Matrix

program ownership, and the like. Several large stakeholder groups filled in their respective portion of the RACI and the information was then collated and discussed as a larger group. Several meetings were required in order to sort through all of the items. This did give the organization a good start on implementing a new, globally encompassing organizational design.

When using this tool make it as granular as needed to determine how the majority of decisions will flow. The horizontal axis and right-hand side of the matrix lists the entities, individuals, and functions—all stakeholders in the core processes. Note that accountability and responsibility are shared in some instances.

The process of completing the decision matrix following the implementation of a new shared services organization helped operationalize the new model and bring it to life. There is tremendous value in formally vetting the decision making process when a new organization is formed. It promotes communication, eliminates barriers and gray areas, and helps the productive launch of a new organization design.

If the design effort is well-orchestrated, then management will have followed a stable process, created and evaluated multiple design options against design criteria that are strategic enablers, and included sufficient stakeholder buy-in to prevent any surprises. The design should provide a good foundation on which to evolve the organization for, at minimum, 18 months to 2 years and leave a document trail of thinking that will help with a company's next cycle of organizational evolution.

Chapter Six Note

1. Workforce Productivity Study. Pritchett & Associates. 1994.

Chapter Seven

Calibrating Leverage, Needed Investment, and the Value of Functions

Not everything that can be counted counts,
and not everything that counts can be counted.
—Albert Einstein

This entire book is about how to leverage the power of an organization through the mobilization of ideas—in order to create a productive and profitable business.

The yin and yang of idea mobilization

Idea generation and idea mobilization are essentially the yin-yang of any organization, be it for profit or not for profit. The yin-yang principle (Figure 7.1, below) represents Taoism's way of understanding the fluid and ever-shifting interrelationship of opposites. While introducing this principle may smack as being a bit on the dramatic side, I like to use it when comparing and contrasting the importance of an organization's functional areas. Several functional areas are responsible for the creation, incubation, and realization of ideas that manifest themselves as products and services delivered to a consumer. These functional areas might include: R&D, Product Development, Engineering, and/or Product Marketing (a blurry line) or what I term the "yin" of an organization. The purpose of other functions, the "yang" so to speak, is to take great product and service ideas and bring these to market. Functions here might include: Manufacturing, Sales, Marketing, Logistics, Finance, Human Resources, and Administrative Services. Note: see a list of typical functional areas at the end of this chapter.

Figure 7.1: The Yin-Yang Symbol

An organization is essentially a lattice that weaves together specialized functions to create and provide a service or product to a consumer. It's good to be aware that each function doesn't offer the same value at the same time to the organization. For example, early-stage organizations generally don't have the funding or in some cases the immediate need to set up and operate all typical functional areas. Roles are blended and one leader might be responsible for a cluster of functional duties. As the saying goes in Silicon Valley, "In the start-up environment, you do it all from designing the product to cleaning the toilets." Determining the point at which functional specialists are needed, how many are needed, at what skill level, and so on, is tricky business. The required investment depends on a number of factors related to business maturity.

For example, a seemingly disproportionate investment in recruiting may be required as a new organization scales, more so than a mature-staged business with low attrition and a focus on growing talent internally.

While support functions (e.g., IT, Finance, Human Resources, Marketing, Facilities, Logistics, and Administration) do not directly generate revenue, under-investment can sub-optimize business growth, scaling, and revenue generation. These support functions are core to the "yang" or mobilization of ideas. Without competence in these areas, the best ideas may never profitably reach the market.

Many leaders believe that "engineering" is, hands down, the most important function. If you have the best product engineering in the market you win. It's that simple, in their minds. Unfortunately, literature proves this to be a myth that defies the realities of a competitive environment. While the best technology, product, or services is a desirable position, it is seldom enough to establish a winning position in the market. And, while today's consumers want

> *"Without competence in these areas, the best ideas may never profitably reach the market."*

the best product, they also want the best service, an elegant simple solution, a great user interface (even if not in the technology arena), relative quality, competitive price, convenience, and responsive customer service.

As a case in point, try this short exercise: choose the function that is most important in this scenario. An airline company flies passenger jets globally as a money-making business. These functional groups are involved: 1) Purchasing to acquire airplanes, 2) Human Resources to hire and retain qualified pilots, mechanics, and other personnel, 3) Maintenance to keep the airplanes serviced and safe, 4) Quality Control to ensure that maintenance processes, food service processes, etc., are rigorous and adhered to, 5) Ticketing Agents who are the face to the customer and responsible for providing a good front-end experience, 6) Flight Attendants who provide customer service during the flights, 7) Sales & Marketing that provide competitive ticket pricing, travel routes, and branding, and 8) Management that oversees and makes sure that all of the functions operate well together and that the company makes a profit. I suppose that one could answer the question like this: "Maintenance to keep the airplanes serviced and safe is job number one. Oh, and competent pilots are really important too." Is a poor safety record the main reason that an airline company fails or is driven out of business by competitors? No, in fact, most airlines that have come and gone from the market did so because of poor planning, non-competitive rates, lack of route coverage, underwhelming service, and inefficiencies that led to customer defection and a drop in revenue. Does this mean that safety isn't critically important? Of course not. It does mean, however, that an organization is a system that needs *all* of its pieces working together in harmony and in an aligned fashion to be successful. So, all functions have relative importance when considering that a successful business must not only invent a product or offer a service but it must also successfully deliver that product and/or service to a targeted consumer. In fact, trying to determine the importance of one function relative to another is a non sequitur activity—it's a misleading activity that tends to bias leadership and skew judgment—both crippling factors in a competitive landscape. I don't mean to downplay the importance of innovation or invention. But great ideas and great products and services rarely evolve and succeed in the market without a suite of

"...trying to determine the importance of one function relative to another is a non sequitur activity..."

functional areas working in unison, all playing an integral role, to move a creative concept to a money-producing reality. It is the yin-yang in action. Taking a position that one function is critically important while another is not undermines the basic tenets of the term, "organization," and undermines the power of "organizational effectiveness"—which is the heart of a successful enterprise.

Like the yin-yang analogy, the importance of functional areas shifts over time as an organization develops and grows. It is critical to understand the value each functional area can offer during the organizational life cycle and invest accordingly—or what I would term "relative investment." I like to ask the question, "Given the current state of the organization and upcoming needs, looking out 18 to 24 months, what is the correct investment for each respective functional area (and expected return)?" This is a simple question on the surface. In practice, it requires an astute leadership entity, deep domain expertise across a broad spectrum of functional areas, and the ability to translate this domain expertise into a value proposition—specifically the answers to these questions: "What leverage or value-add can each functional area offer?" "What is the return for the investment?" "What is timing for this investment?" "How will I know if the correct level of investment has been made?" "Have I timed my investments correctly across the broad spectrum of functional areas?" "How will I know if the best result is achieved for the investment (across all functions)?"

Historically, many support functions have received a "pass" when other core functions are articulating a value proposition. Support functions, such as Finance, Human Resources, and IT, have tended to rely on ratios or percent invested per employee. For example, a ratio of 1:125, or one HR professional for every 125 employees, might be an adequate ratio in a mid-sized organization. This works out to 24 HR employees in a 3,000-employee global company. Ratios, however, create a false sense of an appropriate level of investment. All support functions should be required to, at minimum, quantify investment on these levels: effectiveness, speed, user experience, value-add or ROI, and cost. Cost alone is not an effective measure. Headcount ratio alone can be misleading. Thus, for the traditional support-functions, the value-add metrics of cost and headcount ratio, tend to distort or mask the ultimate contribution for those support functions. More likely, an over-investment or under-investment can occur. Either can be detrimental to the organization and its given stage of growth and development.

While there doesn't seem to be a shortage of innovators and entrepreneurs who can conceive great ideas, there does seem to be a shortage of leaders who genuinely understand the relative investment that is required for each functional area to efficiently scale an organization. This view is based on countless observations of businesses clearly being disabled by a lack of investment in one or more functional areas. Imagine the devastation that can be caused to a growing entity that lacks competence, insight, and perspective in multiple functional areas at a given point in its life cycle. On the bright side, this imbalance creates lucrative contracts for external consulting firms ready to help rebalance the functional landscape.

For example, two well-known organizations, one manufacturing and selling mobile phones and the other solar energy, skewed their funding primarily toward engineering and product development and insufficiently on cost-effective manufacturing techniques and quality control (the yang of the value proposition equation). Both organizations were trying to leapfrog the competition and introduce revolutionary products to attack a growing market. Early versions of their products proved two things: 1) the product concept was great, even revolutionary, but 2) the manufacturing cost and level of quality were not competitive.

Both organizations were so engineering-centric that many other critical functional areas lacked investment. The yin-yang was imbalanced. Investors and shareholders lost buckets of money. Employees lost jobs. Company visions that were inspiring and catalyzing became casualties of competition. Their company names would not be unfamiliar to you.

Determining a function's value proposition

Determining a function's value proposition is obviously the job of management. When working with clients, I don't suggest a ratio, formula, or even make a recommendation on how money should be invested per function. However, I'm an ardent advocate of objective, thorough analysis across the full spectrum of functions to understand the needed investment for the needed return—today and in the future. Like all strategic planning activity, this is not an exact science. But there is a method or science that can be deployed to help make good investment decisions with regard to how an organization funds development of its functional areas. There is a bit of a Catch-22 here. If the functional expertise does not exist in-house to support the planning activity, then chances are the planning result will be less than optimal—which describes many early-stage organizations that don't yet have a full range of functional experts leading the company. Note: having the title to lead a functional organization and having the functional expertise to contribute to this level of planning (Dimension Three) are two entirely separate things—and is the Achilles heel of many organizations. Make sure that the functional leader or participant engaged in this planning activity is a true functional expert. If not, acquire this expertise externally (if need be) for this activity.

Another caution: it's easy to decide to pour money into technology if you're a technologist; it's easy to spend money on sales when you're a salesperson. The same applies to every functional leader. It's normal to gravitate to passions, interests, and propensities. As described earlier in the Three-dimensional Planning section of this book (Chapter One), the health, efficiency, and effectiveness of an organization is dependent on the correct investment for all functional areas. Make sure that one functional area and the contribution that it brings don't overshadow or undermine the yin-yang organizational balance. Sub-par functional investment (not distributed correctly to "yang" functions) can undermine or kill the "yin." The power and success of an organization rely on the sum of its parts. If the Master Planning activity has been performed correctly (with sequenced imperatives), considerable insights should have been gained with regard to the timing and level of functional investment.

> *"The power and success of an organization rely on the sum of its parts."*

Figure 7.2 (below) is the model that I use with clients to describe what I term a "value algorithm" that is embedded in each functional area. The value of a function shifts over time, depending on the life cycle of an organization. The key is to understand when to invest, when to maintain that investment, and when to divest or surgically siphon off funds from one area and move these to another area higher in sequence—more critical at a specific stage in the Sigmoid Curve. In other words, great management prevents empire building or the development of functions that operate strictly on a legacy-based business case for funds. Great management uses the ebb and flow of business needs as a way to rationally re-examine functional staffing, expenditures, and needed capabilities, and uses this as an opportunity to shift resources for the greater good—to provide employee development opportunities—to promote teamwork as opposed to silos and/or the building of rigid fiefdoms. In addition, it's important that the analysis goes deep enough to identify the core needs that each function must deliver on: "current state" to "future state" and understanding the necessary investment required by each function (in support of its contribution) over time.

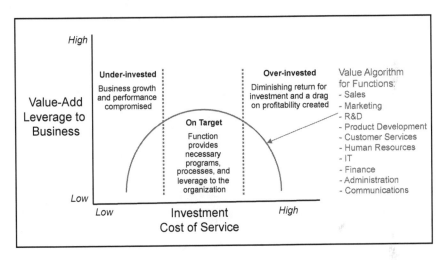

Figure 7.2: Determining Value/Investment for Functional Areas

The more lead time the better when building and evolving functions. Don't wait for the organization to experience pain before stepping up and investing correctly in a given area. For example, an organization has an informal recruiting and hiring process that has been a source of frustration for a number of years. Recently, the head of the company has decided to take control of and approve all requisitions and hires while the organization scales—to make sure that things are kept under control. This is called "failure." With the correct functional recruiting expertise in place, the right policies and programs would be developed as a matter of course to prevent such Draconian management methods as the company head stepping in. In this case, the right time to make the investment to augment a recruiting function is not a week before the organization announces that it will triple in size in 24 months; the right time is dictated by the Master Planning effort and the necessary functional investment identified in the imperative sequence.

Here is a suggested process for determining the value of functions:

1. Create a Data Point for current and future planning efforts and call it "Value Proposition of Functions."

2. Assemble the leadership team. Refine the Functional Areas list so that it's aligned with your particular organization. (See sample list at the end of this chapter.)

3. Have each leader independently evaluate all functional areas, e.g., a) over-invested, b) on target, or c) under-invested (see Figure 7.3 below). Make sure that each leader provides an example in the "Comments" column to substantiate the rating.

4. Have the leadership team discuss the results of the independent evaluation in order to look for patterns of agreement and disagreement. Note the facts regarding any disagreements or areas where further clarification is needed.

5. Have each functional head (or attending domain expert) present the "value proposition" for his or her function to include investment requirements, expected outcomes—current state to future state. Compare and contrast these outcomes (a group analysis) with the Master Plan to see to what degree the functional investment analysis maps to the Master Plan sequence. Attempt to reach general agreement on the required investment levels for each functional area.

Did this analysis and discussion change any of the original thoughts and perceptions held with regard to a particular function or the appropriate levels of funding? Hold this analysis for future reference as part of the strategic planning record and for further refinement over time. This activity provides critical planning context for work force scaling and the development of a location strategy.

Functional Area	Over-invested	On Target	Under-invested	Comments
Sales	■			
Marketing		■		
Research	■			
Production		■		
Operations				
Customer Service		■		
IT			■	
Management		■		
Finance		■		
Human Resources			■	
Product Devel.	■			

Figure 7.3: Functional Value Worksheet

Donning my consultant hat, I should note that I don't believe that many leadership teams have a comprehensive understanding of the value proposition for each functional area, especially with regard to functional contribution at different times in a company's life cycle. This is vital information when investing thousands or even millions of dollars on headcount, capital items, location propagation, and domain expertise. Given the importance of this topic I would suggest significant preparation for such an activity and include all functional areas in the consideration, i.e., hire domain experts to support valuation activity when needed.

There is an old adage that states, "You need to spend money to make money." This statement pertains to company owners who must invest money in their businesses to acquire and maintain needed capacity and capability—to create opportunities to earn the maximum amount of money back on that investment. It is the responsibility of each functional head (Sales, Marketing, Product Development, Research & Development, Production, Operations, Customer Service, Human Resources, Information Technology, Finance, Management, Distribution, and Administration) to help determine objectively how to invest the organization's funds in order to get the best possible return. As Warren Buffett has said, "The chains of habit are too light to be felt until they are too heavy to be broken." In the dynamic, fast-moving, and complex landscapes in which our organizations must operate today, leadership needs to be skilled at precision functional investment. Is it possible to over-invest in product development? Under-invest in sales? Neglect certain innocuous areas of the company forced to play catch-up later, such as IT or HR? The answer to all of the above is, of course, yes. Make sure your planning effort adequately addresses the value of functions—a critical facet of planning.

Generic List of Business Functions

1. Human Resources
2. Sales
3. Marketing
4. Research & Development
5. Production
6. Operations
7. Customer Service
8. Finance
9. Account Management

10. Administration
11. IT
12. Management
13. Business Intelligence
14. Engineering
15. Product Management
16. Logistics
17. Communications
18. Distribution

 **Chapter Eight**

Creating a Culture That Attracts and Retains Talented, Passionate People

*Nothing will kill your reputation in the labor market faster than
doing a great job advertising a work experience you don't deliver.*
—David Ogilvy

"Wanted: unmotivated, unskilled, dispassionate workers with no future. Please apply here." This might be the recruiting slogan for a Middle East suicide bombers' organization, but I bet you'll never see this ad posted by a competitive business—anywhere in the world. Why? People are the organization, so to speak, in the "information age." Every night the organization goes home. If the employees don't come back, the organization ceases to exist. Unless you're dealing in gold, platinum, or precious gems, the greatest investment will always be employees. As such, it is just common sense that if leadership creates a culture that protects and nurtures this investment, that return can be phenomenal.

My intention is to write a sequel to *Beyond Genius, Innovation &
Luck* specifically targeted at the development and evolution of company culture. I have some strong thoughts on this topic, having supported

many organizations that were undergoing leader transitions, mergers and acquisitions, and workforce turmoil—all rooted in profound "change" events. However, in writing this book, I realized that culture is so incredibly vital to the discussion that I needed to include it here, even if in condensed form.

So, let me tee up the conversation of culture. Hard-core technologists and engineers tend to roll their eyes when the topic of culture comes up. That's too bad because there is definitive data, as never before, demonstrating that culture does influence shareholder value, attraction, and retention of key talent—and it can be the difference between competing and winning and never becoming a serious competitive threat. Culture is the manifestation of all of the things that we have discussed thus far and more: leadership traits, purpose, teaming, values, and so on. I'll start with a definition of culture and then move into what is considered to be a cultural nirvana: the Employer of Choice company.

What is company culture?

A company's culture consists of those unique characteristics that make up the organization: how people interact with one another and in work groups, its core values (how leaders and employees actually behave), the overarching philosophy and tenets that guide the organization, rules about how people get along (written down or not), the general sensory feeling or climate of the environment (are you greeted by a security guard when you walk in the door or step into a product showcase?), and the general shared view about the way things work. Bill Hewlett and David Packard created a company that was founded on the famous "HP Way." The founders went to great lengths to canonize this prescriptive cultural approach in the environment. One tenet of the HP Way was "no layoffs."

Bill and David wanted to send the message that people mattered. When times got tough, all other measures would be exercised before heads would be cut. Layoffs didn't begin to occur regularly at HP until the reins of the company were handed off to the third- and fourth-generation leaders, Carly Fiorina and Mark Hurd, respectively. It seems that some people forgot to study the HP Way document before assuming command.

"One tenet of the HP Way was 'no layoffs'."

While at BEA Systems, Bill Coleman, then CEO, was keenly interested in imprinting the company culture on new leaders and employees as the organization scaled. At that time, BEA had successfully grown to a $1-billion business (3,100 employees in 23 countries) and was now ready to make the leap to exponential growth. Here is how Bill described the BEA Systems culture:

▷ Customers come first

▷ Teamwork within and across teams

▷ Individual empowerment

▷ Agree or disagree, but commit

▷ Respect and know the competition

▷ Good enough isn't acceptable

▷ Prompt action, prompt response

Why is culture important?

Culture exists. It's real and affects the daily operation of any enterprise whether it is acknowledged or not. Culture combined with an agenda (a mission) creates what I term "organizational momentum." This momentum can work for or against what leadership wants to accomplish.

It's great when the workforce is focused and working in unison, but it can be a nightmare when leadership wants to shift the agenda or direction and do so with some degree of finesse. Cultural momentum is probably the most important and the least-recognized factor in the formulation and execution of strategy. To further explain this point, I will share an experience that dramatically shaped my own perceptions.

At 10 years of age, I watched the movie, *Moses*, a reenactment of the time of Pharaohs and pyramids. One of the tasks of pyramid construction was to quarry large, multi-ton blocks of stone and then haul these to the construction site. One scene showed how they actually moved a stone to the site. Probably some 1,000 slaves were pulling on a rope attached to a block of stone that was easily the size of a small house. To help the block move across the ground with less friction, workers called runners moved smooth roller logs continuously to the front of the block. The huge block was

"...never jump out in front of cultural momentum. [You] will get run over in a heartbeat."

moving at a snail's pace. When one of the workers tripped and got his foot caught, no one batted an eye as that 20-ton stone block slowly crushed the life out of him, inch by inch. As a child, I thought how cruel society must have been back then. As an adult, I realized that this was my first lesson in organizational theory. Because of the size of this pyramid-building operation—which included 1,000 workers pulling on a rope, no one individual or group of individuals could have possibly coordinated stopping the stone quickly enough to save the life of the log runner. Even the head of construction did not have the power to stop the block. There were just too many people involved to instantaneously halt the activity.

With the increased size of the organization comes increased momentum. Whenever you get a bunch of people all working toward some common goal, you will find momentum. That kind of momentum (it's amorphous—you can't touch it or feel it) cannot be stopped on a dime or quickly redirected. In this regard, organizations have a mindless nature to them. You can bet that in the typical large corporation of, let's say, 20,000 employees, regardless of what management wants to change, the organization's momentum will always resist efforts to redirect or change it. That's why I tell leaders—and especially a new leader—to never jump out in front of cultural momentum. They will get run over in a heartbeat.

I related this story to an executive of a manufacturing organization several years ago. While I was telling the story he was continually nodding his head in agreement. At the end of the story he said, "I've never known what to call it, but let me give you an example of cultural momentum. Years back I was given an assignment to take over a manufacturing division of a company. One of my first actions was to oppose the completion of a product that had been under development for years. It just didn't make sense to me that they take this product to market. In many respects, it was already obsolete. Against the best advice of my direct reports, engineers two and three levels down in the organization and some peer managers, I killed the project. Guess what? I got fired from that job and moved over to this staff job. I'm in the executive penalty box. I think I got run over by cultural momentum." The lesson here is that no one, regardless of position, is immune to the powerful effects of momentum that are inherent in culture.

Culture creates a company context

Culture is important because it provides a context that sets expectations, gives leaders and managers a firm basis for decision making (hypercritical in 24/7 globally distributed organizations), defines the company's brand internally and externally, and creates a behavioral sandbox, so to speak, in which all employees play (interact). To the second point above, "a firm basis for decision making," as organizations scale, decision making becomes more and more distributed. Leaders and managers, spread across time zones, geographies, and cultures, are making constant real-time decisions. A well-defined and inculcated culture is the most efficient way to ensure that these decisions are in fact being made in context and aligned with the best interests of the organization (and the situation). I remember discussing this point with a CEO of a mid-sized global company. He was the founder of this successful manufacturing organization with a 15-year history. He said, "I know every manager in this company and he or she knows how I think. I don't see any issues here." Not so fast. Is it really possible for a CEO to know all 630 managers in a global organization well enough so that each manager completely understands the CEO's intent and the type of decision that he would make in any given situation? You can draw your own conclusion here. This CEO didn't believe that culture needed to be explicitly documented and communicated. I can tell you that his communication style left a lot to be desired. I also believe that a lack of astute cultural management had created intrinsic performance problems and was a reason that this organization was crawling with consulting support.

It's typical for an early-stage organization that hasn't given much formal thought to culture to wind up with 200 employees and market traction and then become confronted with urgent scaling needs. The market is developing, investors are putting up cash, and it's apparent that the conditions are right for liftoff. Leaders then realize—whoa— if we double our size in a year or two we had better be laser-focused on whom we hire, how we grow, and how we make decisions, or we might destroy our unique culture and the magic sauce that got us to this point. This scenario is not such a rare occurrence and even more typical in founder-led organizations (discussed below). Another scenario I've witnessed is when a founder (or group of founders) builds a company that took 10 years to reach $150 million in revenue. Then, seemingly overnight, the company is confronted with doubling or tripling in size in two years as the market niche develops. Business as usual is not the solution; ironically this is when founders tend to depart or begin to withdraw from organizations that they birthed. When the founder leaves, the unique traits (cultural elements) of that founder go with him and are not replicable in the environment by incoming leadership. The trick here is to recognize this event as a serious acculturation issue and address it swiftly and diligently in a formal cultural transition. Otherwise, the environment going forward, with unstable or ill-defined culture elements, will undoubtedly translate to inefficiencies in the organization at large. The Hubble Syndrome raises its ugly head once again.

"Company values...are the ultimate governing tool."

Are company values important?

Company values, an element of company culture, are the ultimate governing tool. Values provide a subtle, constant context that lays the foundation for "who we are." It provides a basis on which decisions and choices are made consistently anywhere in the world. Processes and procedures will change. Systems will change. But values are a real constant. Bottom line, company values serve to build a strong, aligned team that translates into business success and shareholder value. And company values provide the ultimate scaling tool. As organizations grow in size and number of employees, values are the glue that holds the organization together and ensures that a winning team, one team, prevails.

An example of company values: BEA Systems

The three founders of BEA Systems, Bill Coleman, Edward Scott, and Alfred Chuang (thus BEA), built the organization on seven core values. Bill noted that these were BEA's version of the HP Way. The values were:

1.   Customer issues transcend all others

2.   Quality products that work and meet our customer's needs

3.   Uncompromising business ethics

4.   Treat all others with respect and humility

5.   Make and take commitments seriously; commit only what we can deliver; never mislead customers, partners, or colleagues

6.   Focus on innovation and competitiveness, not just innovation for innovation's sake

7.   Willingness to embrace change

As Bill (then CEO) prepared the organization for anticipated exponential global scaling, he noted concern about the degree to which the company's leaders and employees in fact embraced these values. He observed, "We have done a lot of growing over the past couple of years. We may have strayed a bit from these original values. So, it's important to refresh our position before we go through another growth spurt." Bill knew that as BEA scaled from 3,100 employees to 5,000 or more that considerable strain would be placed on the organization in many forms. A key to keeping leadership, management, and employees aligned and on the same page—and on the same team—would be to make sure that these company values were deeply embedded into the fabric of the organization.

Bill asked me to conduct a values assessment. We learned that company values 1, 2, 3, and 6 were alive and well. Most employees, managers, and leaders could cite evidence of these behaviors in the course of day-to-day activity. A portion of value #5 was a problem. At the executive level, there was a tendency to overcommit and under-deliver. This created a rift in the leadership ranks. When an executive did under-deliver, there usually was no consequence for missing the commitment—or even a performance improvement discussion. In addition, value #7 was problematic. It was clear that the functional executives were entrenched and resistive of discussions that might impact their respective fiefdoms in support of a scaling plan. No one wanted to give up power or directly discuss potential changes in strategy and organization design. This was the original executive team that essentially took the company from nothing to $1 billion in revenue, 3,100 employees, private to public, and a stellar pure play in the enterprise software business. It took the fortitude and dedication of the CEO, Bill, to first resell the importance of company culture and values to his leadership team. Then, the executive group invested considerable time and energy to align the balance of the organization. We used the GE model, popularized by Jack Welch, to create an approach for what we were trying to achieve with the cultural alignment effort (Figure 8.1, below).

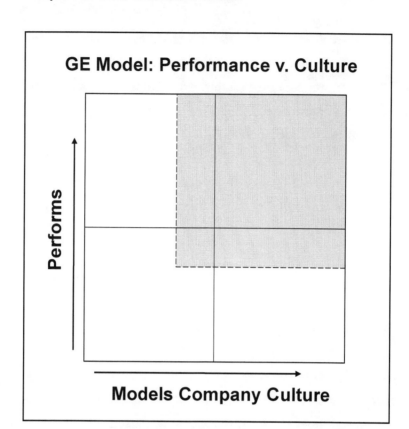

Figure 8.1: GE Performance v. Culture Model

Welch's basic premise was that leaders and employees needed to exhibit both capabilities: meet or exceed performance requirements, and model GE's very prescriptive culture (shaded area of diagram). If an employee was somehow hitting the numbers but wasn't exhibiting GE values, then there was no future for that individual at GE. As Welch inferred, this individual was likely destructive to teams and in-it-for-herself and not acting in the best interests of the company. Alternatively, an employee who appeared to model the GE values but couldn't consistently perform created drag on the team and the company. Certainly a time investment would be made to help the employee improve performance, but if achievement remained low then this individual would be jettisoned from the environment. Just about every organization can identify high-performing egomaniacs located somewhere in the environment. GE took an aggressive stance on this and weeded these people out, stating that countercultural behavior was toxic to the company's long-term viability.

What is the leader's role in developing and sustaining culture?

While the top-ranking officer in the company, the CEO, sets the tone and foundation for culture, every employee is responsible for embracing and helping to sustain the culture. Employees are cultural messengers internally and externally—the best branding activity that any company has at its disposal. There is a proviso here: employees experience culture locally. Thus, a company culture can't be so distinct and inflexible as to counteract or be in conflict with local culture. This has become a major challenge for local or super-regional companies that migrate into the global enterprise landscape.

As we discussed in Chapter Four, the leadership team needs to be completely on board and aligned when it comes to culture. Why? Employees learn and embrace culture by listening to and watching what leaders say and do. If leadership isn't completely aligned ideologically and behaviorally, then you can bet the organization doesn't have a cohesive culture—and will ultimately experience the negative effects of such a condition.

What is an Employer of Choice culture?

It was the mid-1980s when I first saw company communications that hinted of the impending "war for talent." As the competitive landscape had intensified in many business arenas, it became clear that the last bastion of competitive differentiation was really "talent." Organizations that could attract and keep the best talent had an edge—a competitive edge—and this competitive differentiation became a predictor of which organizations would win in the labor market. During this time, I had the opportunity while working with Raychem Corporation to conduct global research (using internal and external consultants to support the effort), specifically looking for the key elements that drove the optimal environment, a differentiating environment that would in fact facilitate the attraction and retention of talent over the competition. What we learned was quite amazing:

1. There were 22 elements that we could separate out as distinct drivers of employee satisfaction in the work environment (Figure 8.2). This research, conducted in March of 1995, included 35 global companies across 9 hi-tech, manufacturing, and service industries.

2. Not all drivers were of equal importance. In other words, a company needed to address or satisfy these drivers in a manner relative to the competition and local venue—but not necessarily be exceptional in all of the elements. Some 14 of the 22 elements were what we termed satisfaction drivers.

3. The remaining 8 elements of the 22, however, appeared to be the holy grail of employee motivation—we termed these excitement drivers (highlighted in gray). Here, a company could differentiate from the competition and create a brand that appeared to offer considerable leverage in the "war for talent." The top 8 "excite" drivers were: 1) corporate growth, 2) a clear sense of direction, 3) recognition for contribution, 4) bonus opportunities, 5) challenging and empowered job, 6) encouragement of innovation,

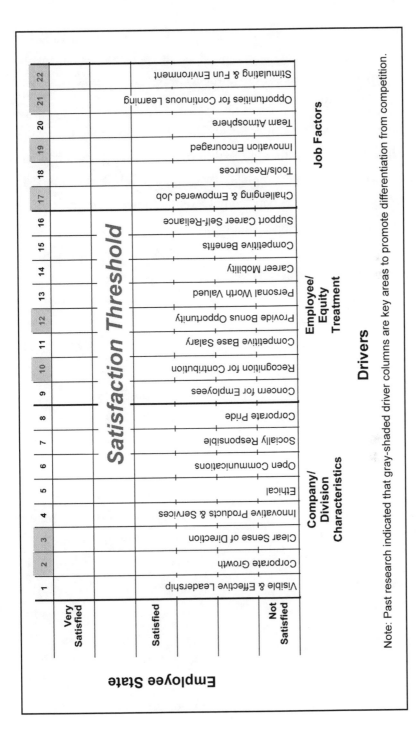

Figure 8.2: Employee Satisfaction and Excitement Drivers

7) opportunities for continuous learning, and 8) stimulating and fun environment. These 8 provided leverage only as long as the satisfaction drivers (14 in number) were at a threshold relative to or above the competition.

A number of years later academics and behavioral researchers were engaged in the act of quantifying the differentiators in the war on talent. I suspect that the term "Employer of Choice" (EOC) was coined in some corporate marketing department looking for ways to gain leverage in recruiting talent. The term caught on. In no time, a variety of organizations started to pop up with EOC programs and related certifications. Substantive research is now available that indicates that organizations modeling EOC characteristics have a distinct market advantage in the war for talent and tend to generate higher shareholder value than organizations not of this ilk.[1] One San Francisco-based company, the Great Places to Work Institute, a consulting, research, and training organization, created the "Great Place to Work" survey. To participate in this survey, your company must be headquartered in the U.S. (or have a large, relatively autonomous division here) and meet minimum requirements in terms of number of employees, locations, etc. A survey is conducted annually. Companies must pay a fee and share considerable internal information. A random sample of employees in the participating companies is also conducted. Employees are questioned about a variety of EOC factors. Participating companies then learn if they have won the award, or at minimum, learn how they scored relative to the survey—with clear areas for improvement illuminated for the next time around. Organizations that attain the award of "Great Place to Work" receive significant publicity and can use this as

> *"...all employees want to do meaningful work that leads to bigger and better things."*

recruitment and brand leverage—and to reconfirm with existing employees that they are in fact members of an elite organization, i.e., the grass is greener on the other side of the fence and you are on the other side of the fence!

Creating an Employer of Choice environment

For the past decade there appear to be four key organizational traits that have been far and away most critical to employees—and foundational to building an Employer of Choice environment. These are: 1) A compelling company vision, something that the average employee can embrace, articulate, and get excited about. 2) Great leaders and managers—people join organizations but leave because of managers. No one wants to work for that high-performing egomaniac referenced earlier. No one wants to work for someone who doesn't cover his back or has his best interests at heart. People want to work for managers who are fair and consistent, and share information. 3) There is a clear career trajectory. With few exceptions all employees want to do meaningful work that leads to bigger and better things. A line-of-sight in terms of career path and related opportunities to grow and develop keeps the individual spirit elevated and minimizes the defocusing algorithm of employees wondering if they are spending their time wisely, i.e., at the right job. 4) "Total rewards" does matter. "Total rewards" is HR-speak for a competitive compensation package—one that might include base pay, bonus, long-term incentive or equity (stock options, restricted stock, and/or cash milestones), medical benefits, retirement 401(k), and other perks.

The four EOC elements above are in no particular order. I've read a number of recent surveys that state that Total Rewards is much higher on the list than previously imagined, possibly number one or number two in rank. Phase of life, not culture or geography, is the main determinant on how this list is prioritized by a given employee segment. Also note that my earlier research (22 drivers) didn't surface "great leaders and managers" as an excitement driver. I attribute this difference to the changing demands of the information age worker and related expectations.

A colleague related the following story to me when she tried to retain a hi-tech guru who was defecting to another company. The technologist said, "It's all about the two Gs: Great and Greed. What I mean is that I want to make a significant, market-changing contribution—to achieve something with technology that has never been accomplished before—and make the world a better place doing it. In return, I want to make a pile of money so that I don't have to worry about where my next meal comes from as I get older. I also want to be able to afford nice things in exchange for all of my hard work." A Swedish executive stationed in Silicon Valley was astonished by this comment and said, "Silicon Valley workers are mercenaries and just greedy. It's all about the money." After some research with a Swedish-based compensation firm, it turns out that the average mid-tier Silicon Valley worker makes less than the average Swedish worker in hi-tech. How is this possible? A Swedish citizen retires with full medical coverage and nearly 100% pay as part of a mandatory government retirement program. Swedish corporations are taxed heavily to fund this social program. So, while the average Swed's take-home pay is lower than that of an equivalent Silicon Valley worker, the Swedish-based organization pays more in taxes for the eventuality of workforce retirement. I have always found these cross-cultural, cross-geographical comparisons problematic and motivated by the wrong reasons—and generally unproductive.

An Employer of Choice model

As noted earlier, the topic of Employer of Choice deserves deliberate, dedicated attention by all executives and should be programmatically addressed in the company environment. The figure that follows (Figure 8.3 below) is an outline of an Employer of Choice framework, a model that I have used as the foundation for building an EOC program. The Employee Value Proposition, or EVP, is "what the organization offers employees in exchange for their effort and commitment" and is at the core. It is important to start here and then clearly articulate that which is "distinctive" about your company's EVP. It: 1) must be noticeably different than your competitors', 2) must be compelling to key talent segments, and 3) can't be easily duplicated by the competition.

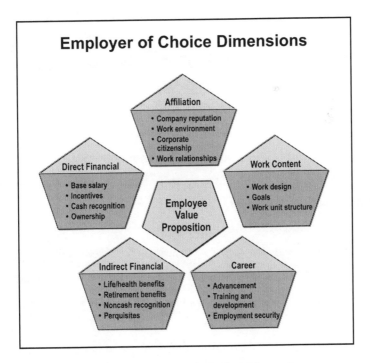

Figure 8.3: Employer of Choice Dimensions

There are five quadrants in this model. Each lists a variety of elements that is important to consider in the EOC environment. A great way to begin is to conduct an internal employee survey and simply ask employees the degree to which they feel that the company is performing in these areas—a survey that unearths proof points or validation on how the organization is functioning. Areas of strength should be showcased. Areas that need work can be sequenced and programmatically addressed. As noted in this chapter's opening quotation by David Ogilvy, make sure that the employee experience that's used to brand the company in recruiting and in other collateral to draw talent to the organization matches the experience an employee will have once on board. A disconnect here leads to high first-year turnover—an extremely expensive and productivity-draining condition. Also,

"Employer of Choice deserves deliberate, dedicated attention by all executives..."

identify competitors' EVPs. This will help determine the proper differentiators for your particular organization. It's possible to build and evolve culture and the EOC environment over time. A huge mistake, however, is to create a long list of aspirations (what you'd like to become) and use these in branding material as though these represent reality. It isn't possible, in my experience, for an organization to radically shift culture overnight. Branding fictitious statements about company culture drops the trust factor on the part of employees—and loyalty goes out the door with it.

Challenger, Gray & Christmas, a large U.S.-based recruiting and outplacement firm, recently conducted a survey with regard to "which perks are most effective in retaining your top talent." Here is the result of that survey (Figure 8.4, below)[2]. Note: I do not consider a 401(k) a perk but rather a discrete benefit belonging in the category of retirement benefits; performance bonuses belong in the category of incentives.

Performance bonuses	78.8%
401K with employer contribution	69.7%
Vacation/personal time	48.5%
Flexible schedules	43.4%
Health/wellness programs	42.2%
Tuition reimbursement	27.3%
Telecommuting	24.2%
Other	24.2%
On-site childcare or subsidized childcare	3.0%

Source: Challenger, Gray & Christmas, Inc., 2011

(Note: Respondents were able to select multiple answers, so results equal more than 100%)

Figure 8.4: Which Perks Are Most Effective in Retaining Top Talent?

Unique traits of a founder-led organization

The passion, intensity, focus, real-time decision making, and mere presence that a founder brings to the start-up environment (all critical to achieving liftoff in the business environment) can, unfortunately, create organizational disabilities.

Founders tend to work in a hub-and-spoke leadership style. It's fast, command-and-control based, and leverages the raw energy (innovativeness, drive, power) that a founder brings to the business equation. However, when the founder leaves or begins to withdraw from the environment (e.g., when selling the company), it's difficult to fill the founder's leadership style. This occurs because too much of the company's DNA (or magic sauce that made the company successful) is embedded in the founder—never transferred into organizational capability.

The incoming CEO can't replicate the founder's leadership style—and is immediately at odds with our old friend, "cultural momentum." Overcoming a founder-legacy environment is a tall order. Usually, the leadership team that reported to the founder isn't a team in the true sense of the definition either; it's a leadership "group." Teaming never needed to evolve with the founder present. Many other dynamics of the organization are likely under-evolved as well.

Ever since founder Bill Gates departed MicroSoft over 10 years ago, the stock price has been flat. Why is that? Hewlett Packard continues to cycle through leaders since the departure of Lewis Platt. I think the HP Way is long dead. I'm very concerned to see if Apple Computer will remain the vital and cutting-edge hi-tech powerhouse that it has become as its founder, Steve Jobs, leaves the scene—a decisive, bright, strategic innovator at the helm. The executive group now left behind will be tested in ways not imagined as of yet. Time will tell. This isn't to say that companies can't succeed once the founder steps away. It is to say that a deliberate, well-orchestrated transition needs to be in motion. This transition is a leap to a new Sigmoid Curve—driven by strategic and cultural transformation.

Summary

The unsaid truth is that any leader who is not consciously managing culture is leaving significant money on the table and putting the organization at risk. With the workforce shifting beyond Generation X (born 1965–1976, 49.6M, 16% of the workforce) to Generation Y, Echo Boomers (born 1977–1994, 77.2M, 24.8% of the workforce), and Generation Z, The Millennials (born 1995–present, 66.5M, 21.4% of the workforce), the complexion of the work environment is changing. The needs of the average employee are changing with it. Companies that are not tuned in to and catering to the new, dynamic needs of "today's professionals" will miss opportunities to acquire and keep good people. Great talent is portable and always in demand. This ups the ante on leadership to understand, build, and maintain company cultures that genuinely offer an EOC atmosphere and leverage the huge investment made in people. (Some additional workforce stats: GI Generation, 1901–1924, 4.8M, 1.5%; Silent Generation, 1925–1945, 35.5M, 11.4%; Baby Boomers, 1946–1964, 76.5M, 24.6%)

As a parting thought: I have watched companies invest significant amounts of money in the hiring of "the best and the brightest talent." Shortly thereafter, they turn around and rate and rank all employees in terms of performance, promotional opportunities, top talent status, and the like. There is nothing that cuts the heart out of the workforce faster than elitism. Net-

> *"Managers appear to be able to dispense with employees on a whim."*

flix, one of the "50 Best Places to Work" as rated by Glassdoor (2009), and listed among Forbes' "America's Top Companies," (2009), is such an example. Netflix prides itself on a rigorous hiring process. Only the best are allowed to enter the sacred campus. If you examine the Glassdoor reviews (where employees rate their company experience), there are roughly 250 comments about the ruthless nature of the Netflix work environment. Managers appear to be able to dispense with employees on a whim. Employees are constantly looking over their shoulder ("Am I the next casualty?"). Is this a highly productive environment? Is this an environment in which you would choose to work? The point here is that many organizations use tactics that are divisive in nature, undermine teaming, and distort reality. There are no winners on a losing team.

Somewhere around the end of 1999 or in early 2000, I ran an employee retention task force for Cisco Systems. Ironically, as the company was engaged in extraordinary scaling (the addition of about 20,000 employees in a 24-month period, doubling the size of the company), employee defections were also on the rise. It was hard to imagine why anyone would want to leave such an explosive, dynamic opportunity-filled environment. As it turned out, competitors were targeting the intact teams of former Cisco acquisitions, i.e., if Cisco acquired company "Bravo," the employees would then be dispersed into the Cisco landscape. The "gold mines" competitors were seeking at Cisco were intact teams (not intellectual property as originally thought)—teams that had worked together before and had brought a product to market (a product that was then snapped up by Cisco). A recruiter would find one or two principals from a previous company, get the roster, and then find and recruit the former team members who had been dispersed at Cisco, saying, "We're getting the old gang back together again and we'll give you guys another opportunity to start a new venture from ground zero in our environment." It was very clever. As we have discussed in Chapter Four, the power of a high-performing team (engineering to marketing, sales to product development, etc.) is extraordinary.

Here were the immediate tactics that we deployed at Cisco to stop the exodus of great people. Proactive tactics to lock talent in place:

1. Clearly define and articulate the advantages of the Cisco culture to employees

2. Increase focus on career planning and career growth

3. Work with managers to improve the understanding and use of the compensation strategies and tools available to them

4. Actively manage talent and make sure that each individual has the right tools, mentoring, challenges, and a good people manager

5. Promote a start-up environment within Cisco with "skunk works" teams, project opportunities, and rotational assignments to keep things interesting

6. Increase management development and make sure that people managers really are good people managers

7. Make recognition a priority

8. Improve information available to managers regarding retention tactics, possible risks, and how-tos when any issues surface

9. Improve company-to-employee and manager-to-employee communication up and down the hierarchy

Culture management is tricky business. All leaders and managers need to be students of culture. If you lose sleep at night over your business, this is a good reason to do it. To prevent those sleepless nights, make sure that sufficient time and treatment is given to this topic. The effect on the ROI can only be significant.

Chapter Eight Note

1. Comparison of financial results with Fortune's "100 Best Companies to Work For" list (1998–2007) cumulative return. 206%: "Fortune 100 Best" (refreshed annually); 138%: "Fortune 100 Best Buy & Hold"; 78%: S&P 500. Source: The Russell Company Financial Investments.

 **Epilogue**

It *Is* Rocket Science

There is surely nothing quite so useless as doing with great efficiency what should not be done at all.
—Peter Drucker

I have been suffering from lower back pain for over 25 years. The source of the pain has been elusive—and was not accurately diagnosed until last week while I was in the last stages of completing this manuscript.

The attending physician, a medical entrepreneur with many patents for his innovations, struck up a conversation with me during the diagnostic procedure as a way to distract me from the procedure he was performing on my back. When he discovered my passion for the effective scaling of organizations (while I was explaining to him the title of my book), he observed, "My partners and I have found that if we hire a few dedicated researchers, pay them survival wages with a huge equity upside if the invention works, we can take our medical device concept, develop it, test it, and reach 'proof of concept' quickly.

Then we are able sell the technology to an existing medical devices company that has already built a viable organization with mature market channels in place, along with all of the other things needed to commercialize a product."

He continued, "Using this model we're able to stick to our passion—medical device innovation—and not get bogged down in the things that are not our specialty and that we really don't do well, such as dealing with boards and investors, developing sales channels, hiring and firing, and all of that other administrative stuff that is bundled in with growing a company. We have learned that we shouldn't go 'beyond genius, innovation, and luck' [laughs]. We stop there."

I commented to the physician that I genuinely enjoyed his story but that it hadn't really distracted me much from the pain associated with having large needles pushed into my back.

On the way home, as I reflected more on his observation, I thought that his account would be a great way to introduce the wrap-up of my book. This physician and his associates had had more than a taste of the complexity involved in building an organization necessary to commercialize a product—and very intelligently tried not to do it all themselves. They were able to develop a business model that allowed them to concentrate on the "yin" side of the yin-yang equation. Most innovators, however, don't have that choice to stop at the innovation stage. They need to build an organization as well in order to achieve the necessary proof of concept (demonstrate revenue generation, market traction and profit rationalization) for their product and/or service. Also, many entrepreneurs are in it for the long haul and desire to build lasting, growing entities that continue to expand the original technology, product, or service concept. For these entrepreneurs, there is never any doubt that they are swinging for the bleachers and intend to build a large, thriving enterprise as part of the scheme. This is where *Beyond Genius, Innovation & Luck: The "rocket science" of building high-performance corporations* enters the picture.

My observation is that building a complex system (an organization) in support of an innovative technology, product, or service isn't something that comes naturally—but that it is usually a requisite for creating a successful business endeavor. Yet, as most often happens, the organizational aspects of building a successful business take a back seat to the invention side of the equation—in terms of time, attention, and investment. In this book, we've seen what happens when great innovation is coupled with an inefficient organization.

> *"...building a complex system isn't something that comes naturally..."*

It can be a quick trip to insolvency. I should note that when I refer to "organization" I'm referring to the capability of people in the organization (the behavioral element) as much as I am referring to the physical aspects of the organization.

In trying to capsulize the lessons of this book in its title, I went down many paths before reaching a decision: The Innovator's Stepchild (how organizational design so often comes second), Slaying Corporate Dragons (how aspects of a poorly designed organization turn into dragons of inefficiency that must be fought on a daily basis), The Hubble Syndrome (how the initial flaw in the Hubble telescope's lens was caused by teaming and organizational issues and not innovation per se), The Yin and Yang of Organizational Effectiveness (idea generation and idea mobilization co-exist, are inseparable, and need to be managed concurrently), etc. These all come down to the same thing: the investment in building the organization—the engine that mobilizes ideas—must be premeditated and keep pace with the investment in innovation. It can't be neglected. Yet, statistically we learn that more than one-half of all business failures can be chalked up to weaknesses on the organizational side of things. And, if you don't build and manage the organization effectively from the get-go, ultimately the organization will wind up managing you. In other words, those neglected aspects of organizational development undermine managing in context, formulating a clear strategy, coming up with a specific blueprint, developing and working in teams, allocating resources, and creating an organization design, etc., all and any of which can become huge debacles that are difficult to resolve once things are out of whack.

It's a fact that, unless building efficient organizations is your passion, there is a high likelihood that you'll build a sub-optimal one—which will, ironically, become your master and suck the life out of you (your time, your energy, your passion, and your capital).

Our business success (our organizational success) is driven not only by our innovative genius but also by the behavioral engine (aka the organization) that is needed to mobilize ideas.

A company of any size is a complex system. We can't simplify the complexity out of the system. But we can use straightforward mental models and techniques to keep us reminded that we are in fact managing nothing less than a complex system and thus make sure that the decisions and actions that we take are, above all else, in context, aligned, and sequenced, and that we've created the shortest distance between our innovation and the successful commercialization of that innovation. The combination of many organizational elements blended with the somewhat unpredictable behavioral soup of the people needed to make everything go—to build effective organizations—is nothing less than rocket science.

In closing, I leave you with a summation of the main themes I've presented in each chapter of this book—each a critical component in the sustainable success of a company:

Chapter One—Managing Complex Systems

In this chapter, I propose that you keep three dimensions of organizational context in mind as you grow, develop, and sustain the organizational framework that is needed to deliver your innovative technologies, products, and services. Those three dimensions are Strategic, Cross-Functional, and Functional. Each dimension is a critical part of the larger whole—each dimension operates in a distinctly different context. It's common for these dimensions to get blended together and treated as one. In doing so, we wind up making decisions in the wrong context, with the wrong input and the wrong decision makers involved. This can have a profound effect on organizational performance on many levels. It's crucial to tune in, tune up, and lead the organization within a three-dimensional context.

Chapter Two—One Organization, One Blueprint

Leadership has a tendency to stop the development of strategic, pivotal documents at the vision and mission level—and then delegate these for implementation. This serves only to introduce misalignment into the organization. It is hyper-critical that the executive team stays involved in the planning effort to effectively translate the vision and mission into an organizational blueprint. From here successive levels of leadership and management will have a clear, specific road map from which to operationalize their respective plans. Companies need a single source of truth and an effective and up-to-date plan on which to base actions and decisions and drive the daily needs of the business.

Chapter Three—Sequence:
The Linchpin of Organizational Effectiveness

Finding the organization's plan sequence frees you from endless conversations about priorities and ad hoc business case debates. The sequencing concept eliminates the age-old complaint of "I don't have enough headcount" or "I don't have enough resources." These arguments are generally irrelevant if the Master Plan imperatives are sequenced—and then all initiative work mapped to this sequence. Resources deployed in this manner are the efficient way to construct the house (the organization) and the most direct path to move you toward your ultimate strategic goals.

Chapter Four—The Difference between
a Team of Leaders and a Group of Leaders

The power of teaming begins at the top—with the top team truly behaving and performing as a team. A company's overall teaming capability keys off of the teaming proficiency of the top team. So, if the top team isn't aligned or teaming effectively, this dynamic translates exponentially throughout the organization. Teaming is not about friendship but rather about making sure that there are explicit common objectives and interdependencies and rules of engagement—and a deliberate and conscious effort to invest in and evolve the teams at all levels over time. Every organization has an opportunity to continually evolve and improve team work.

Chapter Five—The CEO Killer: Misunderstood and Mismanaged Stakeholders

Like it or not, the world revolves around stakeholders. Recognize it, step up to it, and manage it. It's paramount to stop the insidious revolving door that occurs when leadership operates in isolation or at odds with stakeholders. Invest the time and energy, upfront, to get everyone on the same page and in support of a workable

> *"Like it or not, the world revolves around stakeholders."*

agenda. Bear in mind that sometimes the shortest distance between two points isn't the direct route, because the direct route means that stakeholder relationships will be compromised in the process—the kiss of death to executive tenure.

Chapter Six—Designing a Scalable, Stable, Productive Organization

Organization redesign quite often is employed to be a fix-all for company ills. Yet, this solution usually has little to do with root causes and what actually needs to be addressed in the organization. Do not engage in this highly disruptive activity (which is disruptive to employees, customers, partners, and anything having to do with productivity) unless absolutely necessary. Have a well-thought-out plan architected prior to announcing any organization redesign effort. Stick with the plan and make sure to explicitly communicate to all stakeholder entities along the way: what to expect, when to expect it, and how it will affect them. Turn off the reorganization turmoil and productivity loss with a stable, agile organization design methodology.

Chapter Seven—Calibrating Leverage, Needed Investment, and the Value of Functions

I have described the organization as having two factions of functional types: 1) those engaged in innovation and invention, and 2) those that are the machinery that mobilize ideas. All functions are important. Some functions need greater emphasis and investment depending on where a company is in the organizational life cycle and any related needs, e.g., in the start-up world, research, development, and sales are usually emphasized first. However, start-ups quickly increase in complexity and organization need—far beyond research, development, and sales. Don't wait to understand and consider the necessary investment in the full range of functional areas. Know well ahead of time when, how much, and what value each functional area has to offer as your company tackles and climbs the Sigmoid Curve. Consciously and proactively manage the tension, between the yin and yang factions, to build a better, stronger, and more capable organization.

Chapter Eight—Creating a Culture That Attracts and Retains Talented, Passionate People

Company culture has nothing to do with yogurt...unless yogurt and other health foods are offered free in the company break room. Culture is speaking to all of the things that make up the essence of the organization—the touch and feel. Define early on, understand, and deliberately manage culture. It is extremely difficult to change or modify what I term "cultural momentum" once it's established and in motion. Architect the culture that you desire for today and in the long term and put in place a plan to manage to that end. That way, who you hire, how employees are developed, how decisions are made, etc., will gradually shape and build the company you aspire it to become—as opposed to winding up with an amorphous mess of sub-cultures that needs to be rethought and reshaped with great difficulty somewhere down the road. Culture provides the ultimate context for distributed decision making—the bane of rapidly scaling organizations, i.e., if the culture isn't well-defined it isn't possible to ensure that all leaders and managers will be making day-to-day decisions in the right context, leading to the right end point. Creating the Employer of Choice type of work environment is the preeminent differentiator in today's war for talent. Don't get left behind.

> *"Culture provides the ultimate context for distributed decision making..."*

Thank you for taking the time to think through the content of this book. My sincere hope is that there are a few theories, methods, and techniques that you can take away immediately and, combined with your experience, apply in a productive way. The power of the methods presented here can be fully leveraged when used together, holistically, as one "organizational effectiveness" agenda. This methodology can carry you and your company beyond genius, innovation, and luck to the stratospheric heights of long-term and sustainable success. You are now cleared for ignition!

Bibliography

Altman, D. *Outrageous Fortunes*. New York: Times Books, 2011.

Beckhard, R., and Harris, R. *Organization Transitions: Managing Complex Change*. Reading, MA: Addison-Wesley, 1979.

Bell, G.C. *High-Tech Ventures*. New York: Addison-Wesley, 1991.

Bennis, W. *On Becoming a Leader*. Reading, MA: Addison-Wesley, 1989.

Bridges, W. *Surviving Corporate Transition*, New York: Doubleday, 1988.

Brooks, F.P. *The Mythical Man-Month*. New York: Addison-Wesley Longman, 1995.

Business: The Ultimate Resource, 2nd ed. New York: Basic Books, 2006.

Christensen, C.M. *The Innovator's Dilemma*. New York: Harper Paperback, 2003.

Clarke, B., and Crossland, R. *The Leader's Voice*. New York: Tom Peters Press and SelectBooks, 2002.

Collins, J.C., and Porras, J.I. *Built to Last*. New York: Harper Business, 1994.

Deming, W.E. *Out of the Crisis*. Cambridge, MA: MIT Center for Advanced Engineering Study, 1986.

Galbraith, J.R. *Designing Complex Organizations*. Reading, MA: Addison-Wesley, 1973.

Handy, C. *The Age of Unreason*. Boston: Harvard Business School Press, 1989.

Kanter, R.M., "The New Managerial Work," *Harvard Business Review*, November/December 1989.

Kaplan, A. *The Conduct Inquiry*. San Francisco: Chandler, 1964.

Kearns, D.T., and Nadler, D. A. *Prophets in the Dark*. New York: HarperBusiness, 1992.

Killing, P., and Malnight, T. *Must-Win Battles*. New York: Prentice Hall, 2005

Kilmann, R., Kilmann, I., and Associates, eds. *Making Organizations Competitive*. San Francisco: Jossey-Bass, 1991.

Kotter, J.P., "What Leaders Really Do," *Harvard Business Review*, May/June 1990.

Levering, R. *A Great Place to Work*. New York: Avon Publications, 1990.

Locke, E.E., "Participation in Decision Making: When Should It Be Used?," *Organizational Dynamics*, Winter 1986.

McCarthy, J.A. *The Transition Equation*, New York: Lexington Books, 1995.

Mintzberg, I., "Planning on the Left Side—Managing on the Right," *Harvard Business Review*, July/August 1976.

Mirvis, P.H., and Marks, M.L. *Managing the Merger*. Upper Saddle River, Paramus, NJ: Prentice Hall, 1992.

Moore, G.A. *Crossing the Chasm*. New York: Harper Paperback, 2002.

Ohmae, K. *The Mind of the Strategist*. New York: McGraw-Hill, 1982.

Porrass, J. *Stream Analysis: A Powerful Way to Diagnose and Manage Organizational Change*. Reading, MA: Addison-Wesley, 1987.

Ries, E. *The Lean Startup*. New York: Crown Publishing, 2011.

Schein, E. *Organizational Culture and Leadership*. San Francisco: Jossey-Bass, 1985.

Senn, L., and Childress, J. *The Secret of a Winning Culture*. Long Beach, CA: Leadership Press, 2002.

Smith, P.G., and Reinertsen, D.G. *Developing Products in Half the Time*. New York: Van Nostrand Reinhold, 1991.

Sowell, T. *Economic Facts and Fallacies*. New York: Basic Books, 2010.

Sull, D., "Why Good Companies Go Bad," *Harvard Business Review*, July/August 1999.

Tichy, N.M. *Managing Strategic Change*. New York: John Wiley & Sons, 1983.

Wack, P., "Scenarios: Uncharted Waters Ahead," *Harvard Business Review*, September/October 1985.

Wheeler, D.J. *Understanding Variation: The Key to Managing Chaos*. Knoxville, TN: SPC Press, 1993.

Yoffie, D., and Kwak, M. *Judo Strategy*. Boston: Harvard Business School Press, 2001.

Zemke, R., and Schaf, R. *The Service Edge: 101 Companies That Profit from Customer Service*. Markham, ON: Penguin Books, 1989.

About
J. Allan McCarthy

J. Allan McCarthy, principal of McCarthy & Affiliates, has 20-plus years of experience that span 15 industries and more than 200 companies. Allan is a scaling expert. He has also filled CHRO and internal consulting roles with several early-stage to mature companies, including Cisco Systems, Raychem Corporation, SAP Inc., Redback Networks, SmartMachines and BEA Systems. Allan is the author of *The Transition Equation: A Proven Strategy for Organizational Change*, The Free Press, 1995, and now, *Beyond Genius, Innovation & Luck: The "Rocket Science" of Building High-Performance Corporations*. He has a graduate degree in management from Golden Gate University and an MBA refresher (AEA-sponsored executive education) from Stanford University. Allan is mediation-certified and available to help non-profit organizations on a pro bono basis in areas pertaining to the topics of this book as his schedule allows.

Allan invites readers of this book to "friend" him on Facebook and/or visit his website and participate in his blog, which he says "provides the perfect forum to share concepts, models, and processes with other industry professionals and executives in the pursuit of improving organization effectiveness." Visit his website at www.mccarthyandaffiliates.com to check for content and events related to this book.

Allan is available for both speaking and consulting engagements; contact him at Allan@mccarthyandaffiliates.com or www.facebook.com/allanm44 or www.linkedin.com/pub/allan-mccarthy/1/259/864.

Praise for

Beyond Genius, Innovation & Luck

"*Beyond Genius* provides a comprehensive insight into the complex world of high-functioning companies and the leaders who create them. This is not a simplistic view, or random thoughts, but rather a methodical look at the mosaic of influences that impact organizations. The author's perspective comes from his practical professional experience and solid research. I highly recommend this book for those who aspire to lead effective companies."

—Jim Wiggett, CEO, Jackson Hole Group, LLC

"Brilliant people, innovative thinking, cunning strategy, and extravagant plans only get you part-way there. High performance demands balancing the art and science of execution with flexibility, finesse, and resilience, through an effective operating context, within the right culture, in pursuit of sustainable results. *Beyond Genius*…plots the path to high-performance leadership."

—Mark Yolton, Senior Vice President, SAP

"Allan has done a brilliant job of painting a new science of leadership. His book combines wisdom from previous gurus, and takes the leadership journey to a practical level in describing the 'how-to' to achieve results—and build a high-performing organization. This is a must read for all senior leaders."

—Carol Piras, Managing Partner, The Piras Group, LLC

"*Beyond Genius, Innovation & Luck* is a refreshing compilation that tackles head-on the (common) obstacles to having a good plan and a good team, too. Executives of any company will reap rewards from internalizing and applying the field-tested practices that are articulated with clarity and simplicity by Allan McCarthy."

Ziv Carthy, Entrepreneur & Technology Executive

Made in the USA
Charleston, SC
21 July 2013